Nathan Smith Davis

Consumption: How to prevent it and how to live with it

Its nature, its causes, its prevention and the mode of life

Nathan Smith Davis

Consumption: How to prevent it and how to live with it
Its nature, its causes, its prevention and the mode of life

ISBN/EAN: 9783337201029

Printed in Europe, USA, Canada, Australia, Japan

Cover: Foto ©Andreas Hilbeck / pixelio.de

More available books at **www.hansebooks.com**

CONSUMPTION:

HOW TO PREVENT IT AND HOW TO LIVE WITH IT.

ITS NATURE, ITS CAUSES, ITS PREVENTION, AND THE MODE
OF LIFE, CLIMATE, EXERCISE, FOOD, CLOTHING
NECESSARY FOR ITS CURE.

BY

N. S. DAVIS, Jr., A.M., M.D.,

PROFESSOR OF PRINCIPLES AND PRACTICE OF MEDICINE, CHICAGO MEDICAL COLLEGE;
PHYSICIAN TO MERCY HOSPITAL; MEMBER OF THE AMERICAN MEDICAL ASSOCIATION,
ILLINOIS STATE MEDICAL SOCIETY, CHICAGO MEDICAL SOCIETY, CHICAGO
ACADEMY OF SCIENCES, ILLINOIS STATE MICROSCOPICAL SOCIETY;
FELLOW OF THE AMERICAN ACADEMY OF MEDICINE; AUTHOR
OF A HAND-BOOK ON "DISEASES OF THE LUNGS,
HEART, AND KIDNEYS."

PHILADELPHIA:
THE F. A. DAVIS COMPANY.
LONDON:
F. J. REBMAN.
1894.

Philadelphia, Pa., U. S. A.:
The Medical Bulletin Printing-House,
1916 Cherry Street.

PREFACE.

I HAVE found it difficult in brief conversations to impress upon consumptives the necessity of rigidly executing certain sanitary rules, whose fulfillment is essential to successful treatment of their disease. This is especially true of patients who live at a distance and are seldom seen. I therefore prepared for my patients a series of hygienic rules, with brief explanations of the effect of their execution. From these rules this small volume has grown. I find that treatment is not persistently pursued unless a patient fully appreciates the chronic character of consumption and the need of advice and treatment for years, and especially when the disease is least active.

Consumption is the greatest plague of our civilization. I have felt that the public should be better informed as to its nature and causes, for many of the latter can be avoided. Consumption can often be prevented when it threatens. Its mortality has been lessened in some communities by better hygiene, and, unfortunately, increased in others by bad hygiene. I believe that it could be reduced everywhere to very moderate limits if the bodies of children and growing youths were properly developed physically, and if the hygiene of our homes, our offices, and our factories was more perfect than it is. The hygienic changes that are essential can only be effected by a diffusion of knowledge in regard to the disease.

Descriptions of the modes of action of climates, of forms of exercise, of kinds of labor, etc., are so scattered through medical literature that, I hope, by bringing together in this volume the essentials of them all, it will be useful to practitioners of medicine as well as to consumptives.

In that part of this brochure which discusses climatology I have not tried to describe individual health resorts, but to describe clearly how the various climates act upon the human body, and especially when the lungs are diseased, so that a physician who understood the condition of his patient's lungs and general health could choose the climate that would be best adapted to the individual's case, and so that the consumptive could better comprehend what was hoped from a climatic change.

In describing the nature of consumption I have limited myself to tubercular disease of the lungs.

The lungs may be destroyed by other diseases, but what is commonly known as consumption is so uniformly tubercular that in a popular essay the other forms may be neglected.

We hope for much from Koch's treatment of tubercular diseases, which has been announced since these pages have been prepared for the printer. But prevention of consumption must be accomplished as before; sufferers from it must obey the same hygienic laws; contraction of the chest must be corrected as before, and climatic changes will probably be as much needed to promote prompt recovery of strength.

N. S. DAVIS, JR.

65 RANDOLPH STREET, CHICAGO,
November 20, 1890.

TABLE OF CONTENTS.

CHAPTER I.

NATURE OF CONSUMPTION, ... 1

Its geographical distribution. Definition. Bacillus tuberculosis; proof of its causative action; presence in sputa; in various organs; where it will grow; exists in the air. Mortality of individuals closely confined. Access to the body by inhalation; by food; by inheritance.

CHAPTER II.

NATURE'S MEANS OF PREVENTING INFECTION AND PREDISPOSITION, ... 15

Predisposition inherited. Acquired: by imperfect ventilation; by insufficient exercise; by non-nutritious foods; by other diseases; by damp ground.

CHAPTER III.

PREVENTION OF CONSUMPTION, ... 29

Not contagious. Destruction of sputa. Reside on dry soil. Pure air. Out-door work. Exercise. Avoid overexertion. Clothing. Bathing. Climate. Need of systematic physical training for children.

CHAPTER IV.

HYGIENE FOR THE CONSUMPTIVE, ... 43

Varieties of consumption. Need of pure air. Where found. Out-door life. Room ventilation; temperature.

CHAPTER V.

HYGIENE CONTINUED, ... 51

Climate, ideal. High altitudes; their characteristics; modes of action. Need of sunshine. Indications and contra-indications for high-altitude residence; duration of. Colorado and Manitou Springs. Swiss Alps.

CHAPTER VI.

HYGIENE CONTINUED, ... 71

Climate. Low altitudes. Cold and dry: Minnsota, etc. Warm and dry: Texas, Southern California, Mediterranean coast resorts, Arizona. Mode of action of dry climates. Moist climates: Georgia, etc. Florida, Teneriffe, Bermuda, Adirondacks. Ocean climate; characteristics; modes of action. Indications and contra-indications.

CHAPTER VII.

HYGIENE CONTINUED, ... 89

Exercise. General exercise: mode of action; amount; kinds; time. Special exercises: for stooped neck; rounded shoulders; for small chests,—respiratory gymnastics, lung ventilation. Contra-indications and indications.

CHAPTER VIII.

HYGIENE CONTINUED, ... 109

Clothing: kind; weight; chest-protectors; corsets. Mental states. Diet. Administration of food. Milk, vegetable, and meat diet; indications for each. Malt extracts. Oils. Codliver-oil; when contra-indicated and indicated. Alcoholics.

CHAPTER IX.

TREATMENT FOR CONSUMPTION, ... 126

Cough. Pain. Night-sweating. Hæmorrhages. Evidences of improvement: gain in weight; lung-capacity; slow respiration and pulse; cessation of fever, of cough. Need of medical treatment. Duration of consumption.

CONSUMPTION:

HOW TO PREVENT IT, AND HOW TO LIVE WITH IT.

CHAPTER I.

Nature of Consumption.

Consumption is world-wide in its distribution, and is always present. It is a veritable scourge, and is vastly more destructive of human life than the dreaded epidemics of cholera and yellow fever that occasionally sweep over our land. On an average, one in seven of all persons who die succumb to consumption. In certain localities this average is much less and in others much greater. Constant familiarity with the disease has made the world tolerant of it, as the world is not of epidemics.

A simple or untechnical definition of consumption cannot be given. It is seen by all to be usually a slowly wasting and destructive disease. Its most characteristic symptoms originate from the lungs. It is a disease that in its more advanced and well-marked stages can be readily recognized by a physician. Unfortunately, when in this stage the physician's art will enable him only to relieve suffering and prolong life, and rarely to effect a cure. Its insidious onset is only recognized by the most painstaking and careful examination, and often only by the prolonged study of individual cases. It is, however, all important that the onset should be recognized, as it is the most hopeful period for the inception of curative treatment.

The possibility of transmitting consumption from animal to animal by inoculating a healthy one with some of the juices or with some of the substance of the affected organs of one diseased has been studied for half a century and was long since decided affirmatively, but the exact ingredient which made this transmission possible was long unknown. The discovery of this *materies morbi* was announced by Robert Koch in 1882. It was proven to be an exceedingly minute fungoid substance. It can be grown upon the serum of blood after the latter has been carefully purified and solidified. For example, if a minute particle of tubercular or consumptive tissue is placed on the properly prepared blood-serum and kept at a temperature of from 98° to 100° F., there will be observed, in about ten days, around this particle a few minute gray scales. To prevent the contamination of the blood-serum and the coincident growth of other organisms upon it whose germs might be floating in the air, it must be kept in a tube plugged with cotton, which is found to filter the air of all dust and germs. While this is the commonest, other contrivances have been devised to prevent the contamination of media in which germs are to be developed. A fragment of one of the gray scales that have grown can be placed in a second tube similarly prepared, and in another ten days the scale-like particles will have become numerous. Thus a long series of transmissions and artificial growths can be obtained, and ultimately they will become absolutely uniform in character. By a careful selection of the particles to be transferred from one tube to another they will be separated gradually from any other growths that may have been in the first tube-culture. Finally, in this way a growth of one kind of fungus only will be obtained. It was by this process that Koch first separated the germ causative of consumption from all others. After a pure culture of the consumption germ was thus obtained it was found that if a little of it was mixed with water and injected under the skin or into the lungs of rabbits, guinea-pigs, or mice, or sprayed into the air that they breathed, there was uniformly produced in them the changes in their organs which physicians recognize as tubercular or consumptive.

If the substance which can thus produce consumption is examined under the microscope it is found to consist of countless minute rods from $\frac{1}{8000}$ to $\frac{1}{12000}$ inch in length. These reproduce themselves by spores which form within them. The rods are known by the technical name of bacilli tuberculosis.

Belief in their power to cause consumption is based upon, first, their uniform occurrence in the tissues that are tubercular or consumptive and in those of no other disease; second, their power of producing the disease in other animals inoculated with them; and, third, their uniform occurrence in the diseased tissues of the animals thus made sick. We know that the seed of the poppy produces the poppy-plant and flower; for, first, we uniformly find the seeds in the flower; second, we uniformly find these seeds when planted producing similar poppy-plants and flowers, which in turn also bear seeds. Furthermore, from the poppy-plant opium can be obtained, and, when administered to man, it produces its somniferous effects. The reasoning by which we are convinced that the poppy-seed produces the poppy-plant, and thus opium, which is sleep-producing, is the same as that by which we are convinced that the bacillus tuberculosis produces a peculiar kind of inflammation in the tissues of the body, and especially in the lungs, which in time constitutes consumption.

The little living rods can be found not only in the diseased tissues, but also in the secretions from them; as, for instance, in sputa which is formed in a consumptive's lungs. This fact is of the utmost importance, for, by an examination of the sputa, it is often possible to say definitely whether a given person is consumptive or not before other characteristic signs of the disease have developed. It is also of the utmost importance that a diagnosis be reached as early as possible, for it is in the beginning of the disease only that we can hope with much certainty to effect a cure. Unfortunately, such an examination requires practice and training in the use of the microscope, which as yet only a small proportion of physicians have acquired. If at the first examination no bacilli can be found we cannot affirm that none exist, especially if there are other signs which suggest the disease, for they may be present in very small numbers, and may only be found by repeated search. The importance of such an examination is great in cases like the following, which are numerous: A young man of twenty consulted me because he was losing flesh and because of a persistent dry cough. Though slender and slightly pale, he was ambitious and very little debilitated. As far as he knows, consumption has not occurred in his family. The question at once arose, Is this a mildly persistent bronchitis in a person whose sedentary life (a clerkship) has caused a moderate general debility and loss of flesh, or is it the beginning of consumption of the lungs. A most careful examination of the lungs through the chest-wall afforded no positive sign of consumption, but a microscopical examination of the sputa demonstrated the presence of the bacilli tuberculosis. A diagnosis of incipient consumption had to be made.

Another patient was a gentleman of twenty-eight, in good flesh, of good color, full of vigor, and without any feeling of ill health. He was surprised while walking briskly to business by having well in his throat a mouthful or two of pure blood, and by coughing out a little more during the next few minutes. He had had no cough, though somewhat subject to colds. The hæmorrhage caused him alarm, as his mother died of consumption. A careful examination of the lungs did not demonstrate the disease. In the two first examinations of the sputa no bacilli could be found, but in the third and rarely in subsequent examinations which were made during the following two months they were. Unfortunately, neither of these persons could take advantage of the most favorable conditions for the prevention of the extension of the disease. In a few months an examination of the lungs showed plainly its progress, which was steady, but slow.

Consumptive, or, as they are more technically called, tubercular changes, may occur in any of the organs of the body. The lungs are *many times* the most frequently affected; the intestines and the coverings of the brain are often attacked, and the liver and kidneys and bladder may be involved. In children, the glands about the neck are especially liable to be affected by tubercular inflammation. They swell and often matterate. These swellings are usually described as scrofulous. The bacilli, the cause of these various diseases, are to be found in all the affected tissues, and in the secretions or discharges from them.

Not only may other tissues than the lungs be previously and independently affected, but often when the disease begins in the lungs it extends to other organs; as, for instance, to the throat, causing hoarseness and pain on talking, and especially on swallowing; or to the intestines, producing diarrhœa that is more or less severe and often uncontrollable.

The bacillus tuberculosis cannot grow outside of a living, warm-blooded animal, except when artificially grown in the laboratory. It requires a degree of temperature and a kind of nutriment that is not found elsewhere. Therefore, although immense numbers are scattered broadcast by the sputa of consumptives, they do not multiply after they leave the living body. Unfortunately, although under these circumstances they do not grow, they retain, for many weeks after they have been dried, their vitality and their capability of growth and reproduction, if they regain a lodgment in a living body. In all thickly-settled regions, the dust of the dwelling-rooms of consumptives and of crowded places contains some of the bacilli, and is, therefore, a possible source of infection. Indeed, as consumption exists in all lands, in all parts of the world, to a greater or less degree, this bacillus is ubiquitous, and, at times, present in the dust-laden air of every inhabited place.

It is most abundant where people are most crowded together, and least abundant where the inhabitants are fewest or isolated. We therefore find the mortality among those who are crowded together and confined, as among prisoners, exceedingly high. For example, at Chester, Michigan, the percentage, as compared with deaths from all causes for two years, was 31; at Stillwater, Minnesota, during the same time, the average was 24.6; at Jefferson City, New York, at the same time, it was 55. In 1877, at Joliet, Ill., it was 77; and during four years in Austrian prisons the average was 61. The mortality from it in the race at large is only about 14 per cent., or 1 death in 7 from all causes. Almost equally high with the percentage in prisons is the percentage in some European convents and closely-crowded, badly-managed schools. On the other hand, there are many rural districts which are comparatively exempt. A still greater freedom from the disease is found among the inhabitants of mountains and elevated plateaus, and among those who live at sea or upon small islands constantly swept clean by the ever-present and varying sea-breezes. These two atmospheres—that of high elevations and that at sea—have been found, by analysis, to be almost absolutely free from all forms of micro-organisms and germs; in other words, to be unusually clean.

How does the bacillus gain access to the human body? From what has already been said, the chief source of infection will be surmised to be by inhalation of confined and impure air, which has been contaminated by the dried and pulverized sputa of consumptives. This, to-day, is admitted by almost every physician to be the chief, and almost the only, source of infection.

We cannot say that the disease may never spread by the direct contact of one individual with another; but if it does, such infection is exceedingly rare. Rare instances are recorded of husband or wife apparently taking the disease one from the other. Somewhat more frequently have we evidence of children becoming contaminated from their parents. But in these cases, it must be remembered that the vitality of the person who possibly acquires consumption in this way is lessened, sometimes, by previous sickness, or by night-watches and broken sleep, little exercise out-of-doors, constant mental depression, and consequent lack of appetite, imperfect digestion, and, therefore, lowered nutrition. Besides being thus predisposed, the individual is constantly exposed to the inhalation of air contaminated by the drying sputa of the sick one. It is quite as likely, therefore, that in the majority of cases which have been reported as caused by direct contact with the consumptive person, the disease originates otherwise. Indeed, by an analysis of air expired by consumptives, the bacilli are found to occur in it with great rarity. In hospitals where the disease is constantly treated it is not found to occur among the nurses and resident physicians more frequently than among the inhabitants of the vicinage. The statistics of the great Brompton Hospital for consumption is quite conclusive on this point. We may therefore legitimately conclude that there is practically no danger of living and being with consumptives, so long as we maintain our own health by sufficient exercise out-of-doors and by sufficient wholesome food.

It has been demonstrated that what is known as pearl-disease among cattle is the same as consumption in man. Fortunately, only a very small percentage of cattle are thus afflicted. By feeding the raw, diseased meat to other animals, consumption has been transmitted to them.

Tubercular trouble sometimes affects the udders of cows, and the bacilli can then be found in the milk. Such milk when fed to other animals will often cause infection. It has been asserted that in a proportion of trials with milk that was taken from tuberculous cows in whom the udders were not affected, and that was fed to other animals, the disease was transmitted to them. From this latter fact we may deduce a lesson which the experience of physicians had taught them even before such experimental proof existed. A consumptive woman should not suckle her children. By doing so she may transmit the disease to them. It is rare, indeed, that consumption is caused by food, and especially in any others than nurslings. For the latter there is danger in the milk of consumptive mothers and of consumptive cows from whom it has unwittingly been supplied. Only a small proportion, however, of children who are fed from such milk are affected, for, if their digestion is good, the *materies morbi* will almost certainly be destroyed before it can gain lodgment in the tissues. Among maturer persons little meat is eaten, and none should be, that is not well cooked. Cooking destroys the life of germs. Stomach digestion, if healthy, also destroys such infectious substances; and badly infected meat rarely finds its way to the table, as tubercular disease in cattle is not very common. The chances of infection by the stomach or intestines are, therefore, few. It is, however, right that, as has been ordered in some cities, all animals to be slaughtered for the table should be subjected to the most rigorous scrutiny by experts; and tuberculous meat should be destroyed.

That consumption clings pertinaciously to certain families is a well-known fact, and has led to the universal belief that it is hereditary. The disease, as we find it in man and animals, both as it occurs spontaneously and is produced experimentally, has been studied with the utmost care, in order to learn whether or not this heredity is due to the direct transmission of the bacillus from parent to child before its birth. From the facts gathered from these sources we must conclude that the bacilli are not transmitted to offspring by tuberculous fathers, and that, while it is possible for such transmission to take place from tuberculous mothers to their unborn children, it occurs with the greatest rarity. The disease is hereditary, as will shortly be explained, because there is transmitted a predisposition to it, not the bacillus tuberculosis.

CHAPTER II.

Nature's Means of Preventing Infection and Predisposition.

If the bacillus is so universally present in the atmosphere, why do not a greater number of persons become infected by it? Because the tissues in most persons are able to resist and to destroy the bacilli. This ability to resist invasion is due to several causes. If the bacilli are inhaled with dust they are disposed of as is dust.

Lining the bronchial tubes are minute, short, hair-like particles, which possess a constant motion, and which can propel upward toward the mouth dust that falls upon them. Moreover, the interior of the bronchial tubes is covered by a small amount of slightly sticky mucus. As particles of dust are carried through the bronchial tubes and into their various ramifications, the air by which they are carried is thrown into eddies, and is constantly deflected from one wall to another of these tubes. Thus everything the air contains is brought in contact with the adhesive mucus and held fast, and then borne upward and out of the bronchi by the ciliæ or hair-like particles already mentioned. These are nature's safeguards against the introduction of foreign bodies into the lungs. The air that is breathed is thus strained and purified. Very few dust-particles find their way to the lung-tissues proper.

There are, however, other means of rendering inert the particles of dust that do gain access to the lung-tissue, or that cannot be removed from the bronchi by the agencies just mentioned. Many dust-particles that linger for some time in the bronchi are taken into the cells which lie upon and in the walls of these tubes, and are held by them. The bronchi and lungs thus become blackened by soot which is inhaled. In the same way bacilli are taken up, and probably often destroyed. In these cases there is a struggle between the cell and bacillus. Whichever has the greatest vitality is victor, and the result is the perpetuation of health or the inception of consumption. These are the means that nature has provided to combat the cause of consumption and many other diseases. So long as a person's lungs are in good working-order, and so long as the cells composing them are vigorous, it is possible to resist infection by the tubercle bacillus.

The slow growth of the bacillus is another factor that makes it more easily possible for nature's agencies to gain a victory. It is several days, under the most favorable conditions of growth, before this fungus makes perceptible progress. This gives nature's agents time to eliminate or to destroy it.

There is also a difference of susceptibility to the disease, both among families of mankind and among animals. In general, wild animals are less susceptible than those that are caged. Guinea-pigs and rabbits are very susceptible, and dogs and cats very much less so. These differences are very marked. Among mankind the same fact is observable. The susceptibility is inherited, and it is because of its inheritability that the disease has come to be regarded as an hereditary one. The tendency to the disease which some persons have is usually described as a predisposition.

Just what creates this predisposition we do not know. We are, therefore, compelled to describe it in general terms. One causative factor of it, if not the only one, is undoubtedly a lowered vitality in the cells of the lungs, or a lessened power of resistance. Therefore, when called upon to destroy the bacilli which gain access to them, the cells are incapable; the bacilli live, slowly grow, and gain a permanent lodgment in the tissues.

The predisposition comes either by inheritance or by acquisition. It is inherited from consumptive parents in almost every instance. I have already explained how rarely the bacilli are directly transmitted from parent to child as an inheritance, but predisposition is almost invariably transmitted. Much less frequently a predisposition is inherited from parents suffering from other diseases before or at the time of the child's birth. Almost any malignant disease from which a father or mother may be suffering at this time lessens the vigor and power of resistance of the offspring. It has been shown that children born while parents are cancerous are much more prone to consumption than others.

The predisposition is commonly acquired by one of four methods; or, perhaps, most frequently by a combination of two or more of them. Moreover, when the predisposition is inherited it is often increased by the various means by which it may be acquired. The commonest causes of its acquisition are the breathing of closely-confined air, the lack of necessary muscular exercise, the use of food that is not wholesome, and the possession of other diseases of the lungs or bronchial tubes.

It is a prolonged stay in rooms imperfectly ventilated, crowded, and therefore filled with air which is especially liable to contamination, that makes the employés of certain factories peculiarly susceptible to consumption. The breathing of such a close, impure air is often the chief cause of susceptibility among the poor of our cities. They work in illy ventilated shops that are crowded with work-people, and then sleep in small rooms in which often the outside air cannot enter directly, and in which several may sleep simultaneously. Unfortunately, these same persons are often exposed to some of the other causative factors of the predisposition. A legal examination into the sanitary conditions of factories, tenement houses, and the homes of the poor cannot be made too rigid. The construction of a sleeping-room of inadequate size or without sufficient ventilation should not be permitted. I do not urge this only because consumption may be caused if due regard is not paid to the hygiene of factories and houses, but because the danger from any disease is so greatly increased when the sufferers live in poorly ventilated apartments. For example, typhoid fever, if treated in the open air or in a roomy and well-ventilated apartment where the sufferers can be well nursed, produces a very small mortality. But when it is treated, as physicians are often compelled to treat it, in rooms seven by twelve feet in surface area, with a window that opens into a court not more than a foot wide, between buildings, and with a door that opens into a room in which the food for five or six persons is cooked and where they eat and congregate, the mortality is very great. In such rooms, too, consumptives in the early stages of the disease sleep and spend much time. Is it astonishing that under these conditions the disease runs a rapid course and is especially malignant?

A sleeping-room should be capable of most thorough ventilation, and should contain at least fourteen hundred cubic feet of air. In other words, the room should be at least twelve feet high and with a floor ten by twelve. For a sick person the room should be larger; but the greatest care must be taken, and especially in the rooms of invalids, that ventilation is maintained.

Lack of exercise is also an important factor

producing a predisposition to the disease. Judicious exercise—I mean by this such exercise as does not strain or exhaust muscles—contributes largely to maintain vigorous health. By use a muscle is made to require nourishment, and therefore nutriment is appropriated by it from the blood more rapidly and perfectly than under conditions of disuse. As a larger supply of blood is demanded its circulation is better maintained. There is, however, another kind of circulation which is not so plainly seen as that of the blood, and is consequently often forgotten, but one that is quite as essential and should not be lost sight of. I refer to the lymph circulation. The latter is chiefly maintained by the action of the various voluntary muscles of the body. Nutriment in the form of blood is pumped from the heart into the arteries, and from them is carried to the finest vessels, from which it passes for the most part into the veins, to return to the heart and the lungs; but some of its fluid constituents, with dissolved nourishment, ooses through the walls of the minutest vessels into the surrounding structures, and brings nourishment in direct contact with them. This fluid does not find its way back into the veins, but into the lymph-channels. While amidst the tissues, it loses some of its nutritive substances and becomes loaded with the worn-out matter of the system, which must be carried off. The importance of this fluid in maintaining a perfect balance between a supply of nutriment and an elimination of waste matter is evident. The maintenance of a circulation in the lymph-channels is very largely dependent upon the contraction of muscles, for each time they contract they squeeze the lymph out of themselves much as one would squeeze water from a sponge, and on relaxing are ready for a fresh supply from the blood. If muscles are not used the lymph circulation is sluggish and very imperfect; as a result the nutrition of the muscles is imperfectly maintained, they become soft, and are easily wearied, so much so that often a perpetual languor is felt, even when no exertion is made. Fat may be deposited, but the tissues are not full of vigorous vitality that will enable them to accomplish work or combat disease successfully.

In another way sedentary habits and lack of exercise lead to bodily deterioration and want of vigor. They prevent frequent and deep breathing, which is necessary to the maintenance of good health. Only a part of the air contained by the lungs is changed at each respiration. If some of it is allowed to remain too long in the lungs it becomes overfilled with waste matter and ceases to perfectly purify the blood, and then all parts of the body begin to feel the lack of the invigoration which an abundance of fresh, purifying air will give to the blood, and through it to all the tissues. If you will observe a person quietly standing or sitting you will notice that he breathes less per minute by several respirations than one who is walking or otherwise exercising briskly. But in addition to breathing less frequently he breathes less deeply. In both these ways, therefore, the amount of air inhaled and exhaled is made to fall below the standard.

Many persons pursuing sedentary habits still further interfere with the maintenance of proper respiration by constantly retaining a position which cramps the lungs. For instance, we find the student and professional man almost constantly leaning over a desk, and the seamstress, the book-binder, and the box-maker leaning over their work. The body is bent upon itself and the shoulders sag forward. The amount of air entering and escaping is plainly greatly lessened, for inflation of the upper part of the lungs is almost impossible. Moreover, the air passes in and out less forcefully. A considerable part contained in the lungs is stagnant. It is evident that under these circumstances the blood will lack oxidation and vivifying properties; but, more than this, any particles of deleterious dust that may be inhaled are likely, in the stagnant air, to settle upon the lung-tissue and remain unmoved long enough to cause serious harm.

Lack of exercise predisposes to disease of the lungs at all ages of life; to the studious and delicate child who takes little interest in open-air sports and almost constantly bends over books; to the professional man and book-keeper at their desks, or the seamstress at her work. It is also a common cause in all ranks of life; to the poorest working-girl or wealthiest banker or merchant.

Food which is not sufficiently nutritious is a third cause of the acquirement of a predisposition. I do not refer to food that contains tubercular matter or is infected, for, as already explained, this is probably a rare cause of the disease. I refer to food that is insufficient in amount and in nutritive character. I believe that in our own land this is a rare cause, for food is abundant here. A lack of sufficient nourishment aids in bringing about a predisposition by lessening the vitality of the system and its power of withstanding disease.

Some throat and other lung troubles may facilitate the acquirement of consumption. We often find children, between the ages of six and sixteen, who have persistently suffered from enlargement of the tonsils. If such enlargement is very considerable the sufferer is limited as to the amount of air that he can inhale, and therefore we almost invariably find that those whose throats have been thus persistently narrowed grow up tall and slender, with narrow, thin chests, weak muscles, and a pale complexion. These are the physical conditions oftenest exhibited by those predisposed to consumption. And yet this condition is one that can very easily be prevented by the removal of the enlarged glands. It is true, however, that only extreme and persistent enlargement of the tonsils will produce these results.

Bronchitis is in itself a predisposing cause of consumption, for the inflammation in the bronchial tubes causes them in places, and sometimes extensively, to be denuded of the hair-like particles that I have described as aiding to keep these tubes clean. Therefore, if the tubercle bacilli fall by accident upon a raw surface they are likely to gain sufficient lodgment in the deeper tissues and to remain long enough to initiate true consumptive changes. Acute bronchitis is far less dangerous than the chronic form of the disease. Indeed, one might almost say it is without danger, for it rarely leaves a bronchial tube long enough raw to make it possible for the bacillus to become fixed and to develop. But in chronic bronchitis there is prolonged exposure of raw and often ulcerated surfaces. We may make the general statement that most chronic diseases of the lungs predispose to consumption, and that acute ones rarely do.

There are some other diseases that predispose to consumption, most noticeably so diabetes. The majority, perhaps, of those who suffer from chronic diabetes succumb finally to consumption.

A residence upon low, damp, and imperfectly drained soil is also a predisposing cause of the disease. It has been observed that consumption is most prevalent among the inhabitants of river-bottoms and among those whose homes are upon clay and damp or boggy soils. On the other hand, communities who live upon dry, loose, and well-drained soils are less frequently attacked by the disease. The lesson which these observations teach is obvious. By preference no one should live upon damp or poorly-drained ground, and those who are consumptive or predisposed to consumption should especially avoid such localities.

These various factors that develop a predisposition to consumption rarely act alone, or independently. When a predisposition is acquired it is almost invariably the result of the simultaneous action of several of the causes. For instance, how often the factory-girl is compelled for many hours daily to breathe an atmosphere that is not purified by free and perfect ventilation, and that is loaded with the exhalations from many persons, and filled with dust that is raised by the constant action of machinery; how often the same person must maintain a cramped position during the entire day; how often is it impossible for her to get general exercise during the day, and she is too weary to take it after work is done; and how often, under these circumstances, are bad colds or attacks of bronchitis allowed to become chronic for lack of suitable treatment, care, and protection from their causes?

Among the rich we see the young, delicate, slender girl or boy, who has been rendered as tender as a hot-house plant by care and mistaken protection against cold, and even the bracing qualities of the out-of-doors air, too languid to take the exercise and physical training that will give stamina and vigor to the body, and lolling upon soft lounges and easy chairs, maintaining positions almost continuously that prevent perfect and free expansion and ventilation of the lungs.

I have dwelt thus at length upon the causes of consumption, for a comprehension of them gives us a key to the prevention and sometimes the cure of the disease.

CHAPTER III.

PREVENTION OF CONSUMPTION.

IF the disease is due to a micro-organism which consumptives carry with them, and may scatter upon the ground and thus permit of its dissemination as atmospheric dust, I may be asked, Must not its victims be regarded with dread and be avoided? I answer, No! I wish to make emphatic this answer, for nothing would be more detrimental than to inculcate the opposite view, and nothing would entail more hardship upon the consumptive, or his friends and kinsfolk.

More than a hundred years ago the disease was treated as a contagious one, and its victims were shunned and rigorously isolated. This treatment was adopted in Portugal and Naples. Physicians were required to report all cases of consumption, and were liable to penalties if they did not. Consumptives were isolated, and their clothing, the furniture of their rooms, and all that they used was destroyed after their death; the rooms were also thoroughly cleansed and purified. These laws were rigorously enforced for more than fifty years. With what result? The frequency of the occurrence of the disease and its severity were in no way mitigated. Not only does this practical experiment demonstrate the futility of such treatment when applied to consumption, but a comprehension of the ways in which the disease is spread, and of the necessity of a predisposition in those who are to be afflicted with it, make it evident that such treatment is not essential to its prevention.

Since a predisposition is ordinarily quite as essential as the exciting cause, or tubercle bacillus, just as a suitable wort is essential for the growth and multiplication of yeast, we can successfully ward off the malady by preventing the formation of an acquired predisposition, and by strengthening those weak organs whose inheritance gives to individuals an inherited predisposition.

Furthermore, as has been explained, the sputa is almost the only means of dissemination for the disease. If we can destroy all the sputa of consumption, and thus prevent its being scattered about our rooms, our houses, and our cities, we can as effectually limit the dissemination of the disease as by maintaining the most rigorous isolation of the sufferers. To accomplish this object, all who are consumptive must fully appreciate the necessity that they are under of preventing the spread of the malady. For the sake of their fellow-men, for the sake of their kinsfolk, for the sake of their wives or husbands, or their children, they must ever be watchful of themselves, and guard against a dissemination of the malady by acts of theirs. The habit must be acquired of never expectorating except into receptacles kept for the purpose or upon something that can be destroyed before the sputa dries. Cuspidors should always contain water, for it is the dried sputa which may form a part of the atmospheric dust that is dangerous, and not wet sputa. When these vessels are emptied they should be thoroughly scalded. They should never be emptied upon the ground, or among ashes or other refuse, but into the sewers, where the products of decomposition aid in destroying the vitality of the tubercle bacillus. It is not possible always to have access to cuspidors. The handkerchief may then be employed, but should be thoroughly boiled before it dries. This latter is also a difficult direction always to execute. It is better, when possible, to make use of something that can be destroyed by fire after it has been used. Frequently, by consumptives who are confined to bed, small pieces of paper are employed for receiving the sputa. These are at once folded and placed in a small tin box, and before they are dry are burnt by the nurse, and the box is scalded. Many who are not too weak prefer to use a sputa-cup, which should always be made of material that is light, that will permit of thorough scalding, and that may be kept partly full of water. There is little difficulty in gathering and destroying sputa when the invalid is confined to the house. Earlier in the course of the disease the dissemination of its seeds can only be prevented by the constant care of the sufferer from it.

1. The first rule, therefore, for the prevention of consumption, is that *consumptives should not thoughtlessly drop sputa wherever they may be, but into cuspidors containing water, or upon something which can be destroyed by fire or cleansed by prolonged boiling.* This rule should be most rigorously executed, not only that the health of others may be conserved, but that, if improvement and a temporary check has been placed upon the disease in one of its victims, the lungs may not be re-infected or involved at new

points by the inhalation of sputa-dust which, through his own carelessness, has gathered about his room or clothing.

2. *A consumptive mother should never suckle her children, and care should be exercised to avoid milk from tuberculous cows.*

For the prevention of the disease, the acquirement of a predisposition must be avoided by a hygienic mode of life and by the strengthening of weak organs by physical training. In most instances a similar mode of life and training will correct an inherited predisposition.

3. It is not wise for any one, but *those inclined to consumption should never live upon low, damp, or imperfectly drained soil; their home should be upon light soils.*

4. *They should have an abundance of pure, clean air to breathe, both by day and night.* This rule not only necessitates a careful selection of a home, but places upon the employers of factory-labor the duty of providing shops that are well ventilated, and from which the dust is removed as perfectly as possible. In England laws have been enacted controlling the construction of factories, and similar legislation can advantageously be made in this country. The fatality and preva-

lence of consumption is so great, so much greater than any epidemic of yellow fever or cholera, that every individual should feel the necessity of protecting himself and others by providing and using, as far as possible, the best sanitary conditions of life. Furthermore, in all factories or offices where workers of necessity must sit or stand continuously in a stooped or cramped position, so that respiration is limited, a change of position and the cessation from work for four or five minutes in each hour should be required. And yet, how often is the physician told by those thus employed that such a change, even once in two or three hours, is rigorously forbidden by employers who exact the most constant and unremitting labor during working hours! Is it astonishing that the factory-girl is pale, thin-chested, weak-bodied, and subject to colds? or that the book-keeper, the shoe-maker, and the tailor have a similar aspect and disposition? Frequent illnesses might be prevented, and the frequent loss of skilled labor by disease might be avoided, by proper care on the part of employers of those they hire. Such care would certainly be good economy in the long run.

The choice of a profession or trade should be

made with great care by those predisposed to consumption.

5. *An out-door life, and one demanding active, muscular exercise should be preferred.* When such a mode of life is impossible, hours for exercise in the open air should be arranged for and utilized as rigorously as hours for eating and sleeping.

6. *Exercise should be taken systematically and with reference especially to the development of good lung capacity and powers of respiration.* The best results from physical training are obtained in youth and early manhood, while the ribs and framework of the chest are still pliable and capable of being molded.

7. *Overexertion and consequent depression, either of mind or body, should be avoided.* In a word, opportunities for rest should be as systematically arranged for as exercise. Both mental and physical weariness lessen the power of the human organism to withstand disease, and if the weariness is prolonged or excessive it lessens its ability to regain normal vigor. It is as deleterious as is judicious exercise beneficial. Sorrow, anxiety, and harassment lead to lack of appetite, to imperfect digestion and physical depression;

but joy, lightness of heart, and good temper are as closely linked with perfect digestion and nutrition.

8. *At all seasons of the year woolenware should be worn next the skin.* Its thickness may be varied. The entire body and extremities should be thus clothed, for those predisposed to consumption are particularly subject to catarrhal affections, such as nasal, throat, and bronchial inflammations. In a large percentage of cases, they are due to the exposure of the body to damp air in which a sudden and violent thermometric change has occurred. Such inflammation, as has been explained, opens the gate to the invasion of the human system by the exciting cause of consumption. Nothing has been found to so thoroughly protect the skin against atmospheric changes as a woolen covering. By such garments the surface temperature is kept most equitable, and when fluctuations are inevitable its changes are made more gradual. These facts have been demonstrated not only by experience, but by experiments made with scientific precision.

9. *In selected cases tepid and cold baths, especially plunge baths and showers, with the friction which necessarily must follow, are useful*

in toughening the human body and in rendering it less susceptible to sudden and violent atmospheric changes of temperature. All persons predisposed to consumption cannot be subjected to such treatment. It is only adapted to those in whom a feeling of well-being is created by the bath. If depression and persistent coldness is felt, harm rather than good will follow its use. Nor can the baths at first be taken in cold water. But gradually the body may be habituated to colder water. This treatment accustoms the skin to sudden chilling, and the hearty rubbing which is part of the treatment trains the blood-vessels to react promptly after they have been contracted by cold, and to restore warmth to the skin.

10. *A change of climate is often necessary.* In some cases it must be resorted to in order to remove the susceptible individual from exposure to frequent, violent, and sudden atmospheric changes. Changeability is characteristic of the climate of many of the most populous regions of the earth. As such changeability often causes bronchitis and various catarrhal inflammations, which in time open the gates for the ready entrance and lodgment of infectious material in the lungs, such a climate must be avoided by those

disposed to consumption. A mild, dry, and equable climate should be sought. For some, high altitudes combined with these latter climatic qualities are most suitable.

A predisposition, even when not inherited, is in most cases discoverable during the period of youth. This, fortunately, is also the time of life when the human body is most easily molded by physical training, and when habits are to be acquired that may throughout life conduce to health or to the weakening of various important organs, and consequently to disease. I hope that I may be able to impress upon parents my own conviction of the imperative necessity of a supervision of children during all the years of youth by physicians who will examine thoroughly each child, who will compare their measurements and the strength of their various muscles with the standards of health, and who will prescribe precisely the kind of physical training that each one needs to make the body symmetrical and perfect; who will overlook and direct the conduct of life so as to conduce to the most vigorous health and to the prevention of future disease. A beginning has been made in the right direction in a few colleges, and professorships of physical culture have been established. But physical training of children who are unevenly developed, or who inherit a predisposition to consumption, should be begun earlier in life than their college days, and should be equally accessible to the poor and rich. Furthermore, more than muscular training should be prescribed. Advice in regard to the habitation, in regard to clothing and foods,—in a word, in regard to all that will conduce to health and the development of strength and vigor,—should be provided. Such physical education is quite as essential for the well-being of a community as mental education. It can probably be best given in schools. This means an addition to the topics at present taught, and provision for an entirely different kind of training. That good can be thus accomplished has been demonstrated by what has been done in some of our colleges. A most instructive statistical diagram has been prepared by Prof. E. Hitchcock, Jr., and embodied in the "Annual Report of the President of Cornell University." In this institution physical training is required of all students during the first two years of their course. They are examined as to their physical development and strength when they enter college, and then on leaving. For all who fall much below the average of young men of their height special exercises and training are prescribed. It is among these especially deficient students that those particularly predisposed to consumption are to be found. The chart to which I have just referred shows what can be accomplished during a college course. The average physically deficient student falls below the standard of the average American student in almost all measurements and tests of strength, and especially in measurements of chest and abdominal girth; but after training for two years the same measurements fall little below the normal or average ideal, and the lung capacity considerably exceeds this ideal. This is a practical demonstration of what can be accomplished in such persons by physical training only. It is more impressive, for the lesson is taught by figures obtained by measurements and tests made with scientific exactness.

The results of a less systematic development of the physique of youths, which is quite as striking, can be cited by almost every physician. Frequently young men and women of consumptive families are found by their physicians not only predisposed to the disease, but with evidence of its incipiency. They are directed to take suitable exercise, to pursue on out-door life, to protect themselves against colds, and, it may be, to change their home to a climate better adapted to their disease. These directions are carried out, and two or three years later both evidence of the disease and that physical conformation of body which is characteristic of a predisposition have disappeared. Such histories are numerous.

Physical training, though less efficacious, is still very useful in adult life. At this period, however, avoidance of too close confinement and the breathing of stagnant air, as well as suitable protection against atmospheric changes that might produce bronchitis and other inflammations of the respiratory passages, and thus lessen their power of resistance of infectious matter, are of pre-eminent importance. This means an education of the people in regard to the dangers of an unhygienic life, and in regard to the means by which it can be avoided; and, as has been stated, if necessary a governmental supervision of the construction of dwellings and factories so as to insure proper ventilation and purity of air.

If I may formulate a rule which, unfortunately, can to-day be put in effect in a very limited number of cases only, but which it is desirable should be universally effective, I should say that all children from the age of ten to twenty should annually be examined by physicians, and all found physically deficient should be suitably trained and advised of their danger and of the means of avoiding it.

No matter how intellectually brilliant one may be, if physical vigor is wanting ability to execute and to accomplish work that will insure success in life is impossible. The best physical condition of a community has an incalculable money value. The execution of the rule just formulated would surely be of more benefit than can be the most thorough quarantine and sanitary cordons against epidemic diseases.

CHAPTER IV.

Hygiene for the Consumptive.

For the cure of consumption when in its incipiency, and for its relief when established, many of the rules just given for its prevention are applicable. It is desirable, therefore, to consider some of them more at length, and also with reference to individuals in whom the disease is established.

The same hygienic treatment is not applicable to every case of consumption. In the most acute cases, those commonly called "quick consumption," the disease runs so short and severe a course that there is no opportunity for the employment of any hygienic treatment other than what is applicable to all acute diseases. In another group of consumptives the disease is properly called chronic. The failure of health, though slow, is steady. Fever is almost constantly present and lung cavities develop early. The most careful treatment, both hygienic and medical, enable us to cure a small proportion of these cases and to prolong life for many years in most of them. It is unfortunate that more of the sufferers from this disease do not understand how to care for themselves, or for financial reasons are unable to do so. A third group of consumptives embraces the most chronic cases. They are the ones to whom most hope can be offered of a permanent cure. In them there is a first stage, often prolonged over many years, in which parts of the lungs are solidified, impervious to air, and contracted. Exacerbations of the disease occur occasionally, and with them an extension of the area of consolidation takes place. At a later period cavities form in the solidified lung-tissue. In part, the same hygienic rules apply to the different varieties of consumption, and in part they must be varied to meet the special requirements of each. They must also be varied in the different stages of the disease.

I have already emphasized the necessity for pure air to prevent consumption, and I wish that I could emphasize the need still more. It is just as essential for the cure of the disease. We know of no specific remedies for the cure of consumption. We can successfully combat it only by preserving by every possible means the physiological action of each organ and tissue of the body and by furnishing the blood, for the maintenance of its vigorous action, an abundance of pure air. Without pure air continuously supplied our other efforts are almost surely futile. Pure air is therefore, more nearly than anything else, a specific for the disease. It is absolutely needful for a cure.

PURE AIR.

The purest air is found in mid-ocean and upon mountain-tops. It is purer on a farm than in a city; upon the borders of a city than in its centre; out-of-doors than in the house; therefore, a consumptive should live as continuously as possible in the open air, and not in large cities or densely populated towns. The rooms that must at times be occupied should contain air as nearly like that out-of-doors as possible. Those who are predisposed to the disease and those in whom it is in its incipiency should lead an out-door life. Those in whom it is more advanced should spend every moment that their strength will allow in the open air. The need of an out-door life makes it necessary for many consumptives to seek a mild climate where inclemencies of the weather will not drive them in. Unfortunately, all persons cannot avail themselves of climatic changes.

I would admonish such individuals not to be too much afraid of bad weather. Confinement indoors for only a few days will cause a marked impairment in many persons, since the maintenance of appetite, of relief from coughing and night-sweating are so much dependent upon an out-door life. Therefore, advantage should be taken of every ray of sunlight. With feet and body well protected by clothing, they should leave the house, if for only a few minutes. Dry, cold air should never be feared; but moist, cold air should be avoided, if possible. A consumptive may sleep safely with open windows in a dry mountain-air at a temperature closely bordering upon zero, but in a moist air at a temperature of thirty-five a cold will probably be taken, coughing will be increased, and pleuritic pains or other evidence of injury will be felt. Exercise, amusement, or an out-door occupation may therefore be safely pursued in dry, cold, winter weather. During the changeable seasons, fall and especially spring, the utmost care must be taken to protect the body; but every opportunity must be utilized when exercise can be safely taken out-of-doors.

In genial climates and pleasant seasons those who are able should leave the house as soon as dressed; should pass the entire day out of it; if necessary, should rest in hammocks or upon lounges in the open air. As few hours as possible should be spent in the house.

But nights are passed in-doors in all climates and seasons, and many consumptives are confined to the house, it may be, by fresh or aggravated colds or by the severity of the disease. Pure air must therefore be provided in our houses. How often do we find consumptives, with mistaken care, living in rooms the windows of which are tightly closed and the cracks around them firmly battened and made impervious! The air is superheated by a stove. The closeness and deteriorated condition of it is at once noticed by strangers who enter the room. Still the consumptive shuns every breath of refreshing, life-giving air that may enter from without, as if it were a plague. What is the effect of a residence in such an atmosphere? The person is supersensitive to every change of temperature. His blood is imperfectly oxygenated. The waste of the body is imperfectly exhaled and eliminated. Repair of injured tissues is impossible. He has no appetite, and is nerveless, like a wilted plant. The air he breathes is loaded with deleterious matter of his own production, which may infect portions of the lungs as yet healthy.

I need hardly say that in genial climes and seasons the windows of living- and sleeping- rooms should be kept widely open. Drafts should be avoided. This often can be accomplished by movable screens.

At all seasons and in all climates the outside air should be freely admitted to our homes. Where artificial heating is necessary it can be accomplished most healthfully by grate-fires, which maintain good ventilation as well as furnish heat. The consumptive's room should be kept at a temperature not exceeding 70° F. Warm and abundant clothing should be worn. If the disease is in its incipiency, or if the sufferer from it is comparatively robust, a much lower temperature at night is permissible. But in advanced cases, or whenever acute exacerbations of the disease confine one to the house, the atmospheric temperature should be kept as uniform as possible.

Furnace and stove heat is not the most desirable, for they tend to greatly dry and often burn the air. An atmosphere thus modified is particularly deleterious for those who are able to leave the house, as they will experience a more violent change in going from the hot, dry air of the house to the damp, cold air of the street than nature ever produces. The overheating of our homes is one of the most prolific causes of catarrhal colds. Fresh air from without should be admitted in sufficient quantity to keep the air of the house of the same quality as that out-of-doors, only it should be warmed.

The necessity of medium-sized or large rooms has already been dwelt upon. Preferably two rooms should be at the disposal of those who are confined to the house. One should be used only as a sleeping-room. During the day its windows should be kept open, and it should be warmed according to the requirements of the patient an hour or so before it is to be occupied. The sleeping-room should be simply furnished, and only with necessary articles. There should be no hangings or draperies about the bed.

The second room should be used during the day. At night it should be as perfectly aired as is the sleeping-room by day. The sitting-room should be upon the sunny side of the house, and nature's light and heat should be admitted with the greatest freedom. This room ought to be made as cheerful as possible.

Consumptives should sleep alone. Unless the disease has caused extreme debility it is not best to have attendants continuously in the sleeping-room; nor is it best to keep a light burning. The invalid needs all the air the room contains, and its oxygen should not be shared with others or with burning lights. When necessary, a grate-fire may be kept up. Fresh air should be admitted through a partly-open window.

CHAPTER V.

Hygiene (*continued*).

CLIMATE.

As exercise out-of-doors in a pure atmosphere is the first and most important requisite for the successful treatment of consumption, the ideal home for the consumptive must be where the air is exhilarating, dry, clear, and pure. For those who are greatly enfeebled the location must be one that is free from frequent high winds or intense cold. Coldness is rather beneficial than otherwise to those predisposed to the disease, or who are still fairly vigorous. A rarefied air is also a benefit to them. The ideal home must be so located as to afford to its inhabitants tempting and attractive occupations. Whether this locality should be an elevated one with a thin and dry air, or at the ocean-beach with a heavier and moister air, will depend, as already indicated, upon the nature and degree of change in the lungs of each individual. Nor is it possible to find one locality that possesses ideal characteristics continuously through the year. If the disease is changing rapidly the best results will be obtained from successive changes to localities adapted to the successive stages or conditions of the disease. For instance, a physician may wisely advise a patient in Chicago, in the month of December, suffering from an inflammation in the lungs that is increasing the area of disease in them and is accompanied by moderate fever and considerable prostration, to go at once to southwestern Texas. The changeable and inclement weather of winter and spring may thus be avoided, and a warm, genial, dry air and the possibility of open-air exercise be insured. But he may equally well advise that, if improvement occurs and the fever entirely disappears, in late spring the patient should go to New Mexico or Colorado, to elevations of from 5000 to 10,000 feet. If improvement here is continuous a prolonged residence may be advisable. Such directions may be given to one in the earlier years of manhood, but if the patient is past middle life and feeble, or if extensive destruction of lung-tissue has occurred, he may be advised to visit Florida in mid-winter, and gradually to come northward as the heat of spring becomes uncomfortable, and to tarry at various selected points upon the way.

A climate for each consumptive should be selected with as much care as a drug, and to be beneficial must be as perfectly adapted to his conditions. Consumptives frequently wish to go to Florida, or Colorado, or Texas because some friend has recovered at one or the other of these places. But it must be remembered that neither of these places is adapted to all cases, or even to the same case in all stages of its progress. In making climatic changes a physician's advice should always be followed.

The climatic influences which most frequently do good, and the greatest amount of good, are found at high altitudes; that is, at elevations of 5000 feet or more. These good results are not obtained from any one quality of the atmosphere, but from many. Perhaps the most striking peculiarity of the air of high altitudes is its rarefaction. The amount of air-pressure at sea-level is fifteen pounds to the square inch. This pressure diminishes at the rate of one pound for every thousand feet of ascent. The rarefaction necessitates a diminished amount of oxygen per cubic foot; therefore, in order to maintain life a larger volume of air must be breathed per minute than at lower altitudes. A person going suddenly to a high altitude experiences a shortness of breath on even a slight exertion, and necessarily breathes rapidly even while in repose. If the altitude is not too great respiration gradually becomes less frequent, but remains permanently unusually deep. This habituation to rarefied air is due to the distention or unusual inflation of the lungs which it provokes. With time the lung-tissue is increased in amount as well as stretched. In order that the blood may utilize all the oxygen which enters the lungs, the heart beats quicker than naturally and forces it through the blood-vessels more rapidly. This increased work produces a strengthening of the heart, just as work causes an increase in the size of other muscles. Furthermore, the rapid circulation provokes more rapid chemical changes in the tissues of the body, and thus leads to a general invigoration. Just as by habit respiration ceases to be hurried, so, gradually, the heart's action grows slow, but remains more forceful.

These are the most important physiological changes wrought in a healthy man by the constant breathing of a rarefied atmosphere. And these are just the changes most needed by those who are by inheritance predisposed to the disease or have acquired a susceptibility in the earliest years of life. Their conformation is peculiar because of the narrowness, thinness, and length of the chest, and comparatively small size of the heart and thinness and emaciation of the muscles. The constant inhalation of rarefied air will lead to enlargement of their lungs and heart, and, by stimulating nutrition, to strengthening and growth of their muscles. High altitudes are undoubtedly best adapted for the removal of a predisposition to consumption.

The production of similar changes in the consumptive counteracts the tendency of the disease to produce contraction of the lungs and a narrow and thin chest. If consumption is in a quiescent state, the enlargement of the lungs which the inhalation of rarefied air produces compensates for the permanent consolidation and destruction of parts of them. The inflation of the lungs causes the walls of the air-spaces to be stretched and made thin. This prevents their becoming congested, and thus reduces the danger of extension of inflammation along the borders of the affected areas. The habitual imperfect expansion of the chest and diminished vitality of all tissues which the disease produces cause a wasting and weakening of the muscles of respiration. Furthermore, it leads to a slow lymph-circulation, and one that is especially slow in the lungs. But the involuntary deep and full respiration which the breathing of thin air enforces necessarily exercises, and thereby strengthens and enlarges, the respiratory muscles. The breathing once more of pure air and the invigorated circulation aid this change by invigorating the tissues and stimulating them to a better degree of nutrition. The involuntary full expansion and contraction of the lungs in respiration cause a more rapid lymph-circulation, and, as it is chiefly by the lymphatic vessels that inflammatory exudates are removed, a diminution of the swelling and thickening of the tissues about the areas of consolidation is produced. These changes in the size of the lungs and chest and its muscles will take place most rapidly and perfectly in the years of youth and early manhood. In those who are more than thirty-five or forty the change will be very imperfectly wrought. If the disease has progressed so far as to destroy the greater part of the lung-tissue, a permanent shortness of breath and consequent distress will be experienced at high altitudes. Moreover, if the consumptive has much fever it will be aggravated by going into a a rarefied atmosphere, and harm rather than good will ensue.

The breathing of a rarefied air has a powerful effect also upon the nervous system. At first it is invigorated and made more active. An elevation of more than ten thousand feet will cause, in many persons, wakefulness, involuntary muscular twitching, and aching. Some individuals are more susceptible to this nervous excitement than others. To most, and to those especially who are naturally languid and nerveless, it gives a healthy tone and energy; provokes them to exercise; promotes a feeling of light-heartedness and hopefulness; increases the appetite, and stimulates to a better degree of nutrition. These are excellent qualities and attributes to have developed in most consumptives. But we occasionally find one who is by nature extremely nervous and excitable, and unable to endure, either with comfort or safety, even moderate altitudes.

Thinness and unusual clearness of the air are also characteristic of high altitudes. These are qualities which make distant objects appear quite near to those unaccustomed to the mountains. The air is so light that dust and other extraneous matter quickly settle or are dissipated. The purity of mountain-air is peculiarly useful in consumption, as it lessens the danger of ulceration of the lungs, if this change has not begun before a high altitude is visited. There are few or no extraneous ingredients in the air to cause new or greater irritation of the respiratory passages.

Dryness is another characteristic of the air of high altitudes. In general, we may say that the degree of dryness depends upon the degree of coldness of the air. To this rule there are exceptions, for we find in all deserts extreme dryness, but often great heat as well. In mountainous regions, however, coldness and dryness usually go hand in hand.

While living in a dry air a person exhales by the lungs and skin an increased amount of moisture. It is because of this effect that a dry air aids in removing the exudates produced by inflammation of the lungs. Inflammation is always accompanied by swelling of the affected tissues, which is chiefly due to the presence in them of fluid, of a watery character, that has escaped from the blood-vessels. If by breathing and living in a dry air a larger amount of water is exhaled than usual, a demand is created for a restoration of this surplus to the blood, either by the creation of thirst, which is satisfied by drinking, or by the re-absorption of any fluid that has accumulated in the body, as, for instance, in inflamed tissues. It is thus that the breathing of dry air promotes the re-absorption of inflammatory exudates.

I can, perhaps, best illustrate the influence of dry air in removing fluid from the body by quoting the computations of Dr. Charles Denison. He estimates that at a temperature of 71.3° F., in the dry air of Yuma, Arizona, 3937 cubic inches of water vapor are exhaled. On the same day and at the same temperature, in the moist climate of Jacksonville, Florida, 3073 cubic inches are expired. This makes a difference in favor of the dry air of 864 cubic inches. But, if we contrast the influence of a moist air at the sea-level with a dry air at a considerable elevation upon the exhalation of moisture, the difference is much more in favor of the elevated and dry air. For instance, at Denver, because of deeper respirations, which increase the volume of air breathed, 1,062,800 cubic inches are inhaled and exhaled in twenty-four hours, but at Jacksonville only 884,000. At Denver, because of the atmospheric dryness, only 1364 grains of vapor are inhaled and 10,204 exhaled, or an excess of 8910 are. exhaled. At Jacksonville, 3172 grains are inhaled and 8111 exhaled, or an excess of 4939 are exhaled. This is less by 3961 grains than the excess exhaled at Denver.

Coolness, and in winter even great coldness, is the rule in high altitudes. It is a natural concomitant of atmospheric dryness and rarefaction. Variability of temperature is another quality that accompanies these. But in a dry air coldness and variability are not felt by the human organism as in a moist one. A moist air causes a rapid withdrawal of temperature from the surface of the body, therefore a variation of five degrees in such an air will produce a severe chilling of the surface and shock to the system, which is not equalled by a fall of twenty degrees in a dry air. Not only are variability of temperature and coldness very little harmful in dry air, but in some instances even beneficial. They provoke or stimulate one to exercise. They innervate, and thus lead to both greater mental and physical vigor. The experience of every one has confirmed this fact. I scarcely need refer to the contrast of feeling which one notices, the invigoration, on a clear, bright, and cold winter morning, and enervation on a warm and sultry afternoon. Changeability is, in part, due to the diathermancy of the atmosphere which permits the easy transmission of the sun's rays. Therefore, in the sunshine much warmth may be felt, and simultaneously in the shade much coldness. For instance, at Davos the solar radiation thermometer has registered 166° F. by day and 16° F. by night. These differences in temperature between sunlight and shade, day and night, make it necessary for persons susceptible to rapid changes of the kind to be watchful that they do not take cold.

A cold air benefits those whose lung capacity is small and needs increasing otherwise than by stimulating to greater physical exertion. Cold air, when warmed, expands. Therefore, when breathed and warmed in the lungs, it tends to dilate them. That this is a fact is demonstrable by measuring with a spirometer in winter the lung-capacity of a person breathing an artificially-warmed air and the capacity of the same lungs after the person has inhaled a few breaths of cold air at the open door. The variation in capacity is considerable.

Since an out-door life is so essential to the consumptive, a home should always be chosen, no matter whether in the mountains or lowlands, where there is the most continuous and unvarying sunshine. It tempts to life in the fields and woods. Moreover, for the consumptive, it is further useful, since it causes more frequent and deeper respiration than will be practiced in the dark or shade. Sunshine always promotes cheerfulness and hopefulness,—mental qualities very essential to an invalid.

Mountain-land is, almost without exception, well drained. The deleterious influence of a residence on damp and imperfectly-drained soil has already been pointed out.

Living in high altitudes usually necessitates hill-climbing. I have already shown that no exercise is better calculated to enlarge the lungs and chest and strengthen the heart and muscles of respiration.

In high altitudes atmospheric oxygen is absorbed more rapidly than at low levels, and carbonic-acid gas is also more easily disengaged from the blood and exhaled by the lungs. This is a quality of much importance to those in whom the lungs are contracted, and in whom, therefore, these essential respiratory changes are diminished, for it in part compensates for the imperfect respiration which the disease has produced.

It thus appears that almost every factor of mountain climates is adapted to the prevention and amelioration of consumption. Unfortunately, they are not adapted to every case.

High altitudes are best adapted (1) to persons in whom true consumption has not yet started, or has only just begun. 2. To persons whose chests have been imperfectly developed and the predisposition acquired, providing they are in the periods of youth or early adult life. Later than this the chest becomes so rigid and its bones so hard that it can be molded and enlarged only to a very limited extent. 3. To persons in whom the disease is well developed, providing they are still moderately vigorous and free from fever. Of this class the individuals most benefited are those in whom the disease is developing very slowly, and who are still young. 4. To persons suffering from any variety of the disease, providing the mountains are visited while the malady is in a quiescent state.

High altitudes do harm (1) to those consumptives who are past middle life and feeble; (2) to those suffering with an active fever; (3) to those with large cavities in both lungs; (4) to those who are having very profuse hæmorrhages, which may be due to dilated and weakened arteries (aneurism) within lung-cavities; (5) to those whose lungs are so far consolidated as to make it impossible to perform properly the respiratory functions in a rarefied atmosphere.

No climatic change will do much good if the consumptive does not force himself to take all the active exercise out-of-doors that is possible. A person whose lungs are little affected, if he sits constantly about a hotel or boarding-house, and broods and mopes, will be little helped; but a person whose lungs are badly affected, who has the will, the energy, and the perseverance, and takes all the exercise possible in the open air, will often be restored to vigorous health.

To produce an arrest of the disease and marked improvement, a residence in high altitudes of at least six months is essential for most cases of consumption; and for all persons in whose lungs there are large cavities, or other actively progressive or extensive lesions, a residence of two or three years is essential. For the majority it is not possible, after checking the disease, to return to low altitudes and old habits of life without causing a recurrence of the malady. Therefore, a permanent residence in a locality that is found beneficial is always the best. When this is impossible, periodical returns to high altitudes for six months at a time will often hold the disease in check, and even sometimes produce permanent cure.

It has been my object to so describe the climatic elements of a high-altitude resort that each consumptive or his physician can make a choice of location for *themselves*. Unfortunately, in the eastern part of the United States there are no high altitudes that can be utilized. There are many most delightful spots of moderate altitude, of from 2000 to 3000 feet. Several peaks in the Appalachian Range rise above 8000 feet, but their summits are so bleak and so frequently cloud-capped that they do not afford the necessary elements of continuous sunshine, dryness, and protection from high winds.

On the other hand, almost innumerable localities can be found among the Rocky Mountains which afford, in ideal perfection, all of the elements of high-altitude climate that are essential to the consumptive. The best known of these are Colorado Springs and Manitou. In many respects the Rocky Mountain resorts surpass even those that are most famous in Switzerland. They are better adapted than the latter for a residence all the year round. At Colorado Springs and Manitou so little snow falls, and it lies on the ground so short a time, that there is no period of slush and wet ground and consequent damp air, such as is characteristic of spring in the Alps. The whole of Colorado, and even of several of the neighboring States, is peculiarly dry. Rains are rare at all seasons, and cloudless skies are the rule. The altitude of Colorado Springs is 6000 feet, and Manitou Springs, five miles distant, 6300 feet. These are as delightful winter as summer resorts. The air is bracing in the extreme. Both have the degree of elevation which is essential to insure purity of air, diathermancy, and rarefaction enough to produce physiological effects. They lie in valleys and are surrounded by hills and mountains which protect them from high winds, and whose gentle slopes admit the sunlight with the greatest freedom. Hotels and boarding-houses at both places are excellent. This is a requisite of every good resort, for good and palatable food, clean rooms, and necessary service are essential to the invalid. It is true that, for those who have regained muscular vigor, ranch-life, camping, hunting, mountain-climbing, and exploring are much better than hotel life to insure a complete and lasting cure. Such life means food that is unvaried in character and often imperfectly prepared, exposure to many discomforts and hardships, frequently great fatigue, all of which cannot be borne by most consumptives when they first reach the mountains. Colorado Springs and Manitou, furthermore, are surrounded by natural objects and beauty which attract the visitor to explore them, and thus tempt him to the all-essential exercise. These localities are delightful summer resorts because cool and bracing. They are equally delightful winter resorts, for the temperature is not uncomfortably low and rather invites exercise and a life in the open air. Little snow falls, and it rarely stays upon the ground more than a few days at a time. It creates no appreciable dampness. Almost uninterrupted sunshine may be expected from August to Christmas. March is warm, and April and May most delightful spring months. In both places there are mineral springs of rare value, but usually not of especial use to consumptives. Other favorite resorts in this region are Denver, Pueblo, Santa Fe, Albuquerque, and Las Vegas. It must be remembered, in choosing an occupation, if a permanent residence is needed at these mountain altitudes, that city life should not be preferred, and that the office, the factory, and the sales-room should be avoided. A pastoral life is peculiarly adapted to the fairly-vigorous consumptive.

Several locations in the Swiss Alps, at high altitudes, have become famous because of the numerous cures of consumption effected at them. The best known are probably Maloja, Wiesen, Davos, and St. Moritz. They are peculiarly good winter resorts. Unfortunately, they do not afford good, permanent residences; for with rare exceptions, in the spring, as the snow melts, the ground becomes wet and out-door life is prevented by the slush, and even the air is made damp. When this change comes, those who have spent the winter in the mountains must descend to some point already dried. For the most part consumptives wintering in the Alps gradually descend the mountains in the spring and return to their homes for the summer. Repeated winter visits are often necessary. Those who require as continuous high-altitude life as possible can return when the weather becomes settled, and pass the summer as well as the winter in the mountains. The Colorado resorts far surpass those of Switzerland, because they may become the permanent homes of consumptives, as no violent seasonal changes occur in them. The Swiss resorts, on the other hand, have the advantage of excellent hotels and skilled resident physicians, who counsel the guests in regard to the kinds of exercise adapted to each and in regard to the care that each must take in order to insure the best results. They watch and encourage and guide their patients. Variety in sports, exercise, and entertainment is assured the guests of these hotels or sanitaria. Out-door amusements are an important part of the treatment of them. In winter they consist in skating, sleighing, tobogganing, snow-shoeing, walking, sitting in the open air in shelters, sketching, etc.

As soon as the sun is up, out-of-door life begins. Immediately after breakfast, by eight or nine in the morning, a walk is taken or skates are put on. Some seek shelters and sit and watch the skating or games. At noon lunch is taken, and often in the open air. Later, tobogganing or sleigh-riding to some neighboring village may be enjoyed. Snow-shoe parties and excursions in the woods, ravines, side-valleys, and to various points of interest are frequently made. All the sunlight is utilized out-of-doors.

CHAPTER VI.

Hygiene (*continued*).

CLIMATE; LOW ALTITUDES.

Before the peculiarly good qualities of high-altitude climates were understood, cold and dry climates of low altitude were frequently prescribed for the same classes of consumptives. Minnesota, Dakota, and parts of British America furnish such a climate. It is bracing and, for those who are energetic, excellent. But, while the cold is great in winter, the heat is equally great in summer, and between these extremes are seasons, fortunately not of great duration, characterized by much changeability of temperature and enough moisture to make the atmospheric changes keenly felt by the human body. It is not a climate well adapted to the disease at all seasons or to a large number of cases.

Much more generally useful than the dry, cold, low-altitude climate is the dry, warm, low-altitude climate. Of the latter, we have types in Western and Southern Texas, Arizona, and Southern

California. At all seasons dryness is peculiarly characteristic of these regions. The same kind of physiological effects are obtained from this dry air as from that in the mountains, but not to the same degree, for the effects are intensified by a rarefied and cool air. The degree of warmth varies with the seasons and the location. Southwestern Texas is excellent during the winter season for those who need a mild, sunny, and dry air. It is a region easy of access to those who wish to escape Northern winters and springs. In summer the heat, though not uncomfortably great at night, is enough by day to be enervating and to lead to lassitude and disinclination for exercise.

As a type of the best localities in Southwestern Texas, I can name San Antonio. It is readily accessible. It is interesting because of its Spanish features and early history. Its hotels are good. During the winter it is dry, and the air agreeably warm. In spring, summer, and fall it is not as dry as points farther west, such as El Paso. The latter is at an elevation of about 3000 feet.

Arizona is peculiarly dry, and its air is almost invariably clear at all seasons. A dry atmosphere, at low as well as high altitudes, can be found within its borders. In Arizona and in the eastern part of Southern California we find a climate fairly comparable to that of Egypt, both for atmospheric warmth, dryness, and clearness.

In Southern California there are many very attractive resorts, both for traveling invalids and for seekers after a permanent home. The climate of the low-altitude resorts, which are along the coast, combines the invigorating qualities of a sea-air with the qualities of a peculiarly dry and equable climate. It is true that in the Sierras of California excellent high-altitude stations can also be found. The temperature is uniformly warm throughout them, but it is not great or debilitating. The equability at all seasons is, perhaps, the most notable climatic peculiarity of the coast. It is due to the tempering influence of the warm Japan ocean current, which bathes it. The water of this ocean stream varies throughout the year not more than three degrees from fifty-six. It cools the air along the coast in summer and warms it in winter. The interior desert regions of California and Arizona undoubtedly do much to render the air dry. As in most other dry regions, there is very considerable difference in temperature in the shade and sun and in the day and night. This must be borne in mind by invalids. The air of Southern California is bracing and stimulating. The health resorts of the region are delightful not for their climatic advantages alone, but for beauty of scenery and wealth of flowers and fruits. The dryest localities are a few miles from the coast. Los Angeles is the best known. It is an attractive and thriving city, and it is protected from the coast winds. Its encircling orange- and lemon- groves and vineyards are attractive features in the landscape. Near it are delightful suburbs and ocean beaches. San Bernardino is much farther from the coast, with a drier climate. It is also in the midst of a fertile region. Of the strictly coast resorts, San Diego is probably the one with the driest and warmest climate. The winters are like Northern spring. San Buenaventura and Santa Barbara are farther North, but most delightful winter and also summer resorts. All of these places possess excellent hotel accommodations. The long trip across the continent diminishes their utility, but for many individuals no climate can be found so good.

The Southern California climate resembles that of many of the older resorts along the Mediterranean coast. Of the latter, those which are best known are Mentone, San Remo, and Nice. Hyeras and Nice may be looked upon as the extremes of the line of resorts which border this portion of the Mediterranean coast. Hyeras is warmer and its air is less stimulating. It is best adapted to the weakest cases, and to those with slight fever. Cannes and Nice are less thoroughly protected from the Northwest winds, are cooler and more stimulating. They are best for those who need and can bear stimulation. Those who find the climate of the Riviera too bracing may resort to some of the Mediterranean islands. Palermo can be taken as a type of such places with a warmer and moister air. Algiers is another favorite resort.

San Antonio may be looked upon as a convenient place for temporary residence during winter and early spring for such consumptives as are still slightly feverish, but able to take some exercise, and especially for those who are recovering from inflammatory attacks. At this place they are able to live out-of-doors in the genial sunshine, as they cannot in the North. The dry air helps to bring about more rapid re-absorption of inflammatory exudates. While many make a permanent home in this part of the country, it is usually better,—at least, for all young patients,—when spring is well advanced, to move toward the higher land of New Mexico or Colorado. If they are free from fever, and, as is usually the case, much improved in strength, they may go to the high-altitude stations, such as Santa Fe and Colorado Springs, and here tarry for six months, a year, or more, until a cure is established. Many of the mild cases and those advanced in life who cannot be much helped by a residence at a high altitude may be permitted to slowly return to their Northern homes, providing they do not reach the latitude of Chicago, Buffalo, or New York before June.

The low altitudes of Arizona, its desert regions, like Egypt, are most useful to persons in whose lungs are large secreting cavities, and to consumptives with asthmatic complications. The secretions are dried and inflammatory exudation is lessened. But usually the heat is so great as to be enervating and to prevent much active exercise. Therefore, when relief is obtained and partial contraction of the cavities has been produced, a greater elevation should be sought, where the air is more stimulating. It must be remembered, however, that this cooler and more invigorating air means also a more changeable one, which may rekindle catarrhal trouble, unless care is taken to prevent it.

The California and Riviera climates are useful for all cases of chronic consumption, if they are free from fever, and provided they have strength for gentle exercise. Frequently those who have been almost bedridden for months will in a few days, in this balmy air, so far recover that they seek the hammock out-of-doors, and soon, as strength returns, begin to take the all-essential exercise.

All cases recovering from and with a tendency to recurring attacks of pneumonia or bronchopneumonia are especially benefited by these same climates. California is peculiarly adapted for the permanent residence of those suffering from consumption who are in middle life or passed this period. The equability, dryness, and stimulating quality of the air will greatly lessen the number of exacerbations of the disease or hold it in check and promote a longer life. For youth and early manhood the rarefied air of high altitudes is best, providing very large cavities do not exist, or areas of consolidation so extensive that they diminish the capacity of the lungs, and therefore do not permit of comfortable respiration.

In proportion as there is fever or too little lung-capacity to permit of active exercise, the stimulating dry airs prove less efficacious than the sedative moist and warm ones. Not unfrequently consumption occurs in those who are habitually nervous and excitable. Such individuals are frequently unable to sleep in high altitudes, and are too greatly stimulated even in dry, low altitudes. For such persons the moderately warm, moist climates or moist ones which are sedative in action must be chosen. Moist climates are not only sedative to the nervous system, but also to the bronchial tubes, and allay harsh, harassing, and violent coughs. But it is not always so desirable to lessen cough as to effect other changes; therefore, in choosing a climate we are rarely greatly influenced by the character of the cough. For those more than thirty-five years of age, in whom the lungs are extensively affected, and whose cough is severe and wearying, a moist climate may be preferred. But after mitigating the cough and effecting some improvement, a permanent residence should be chosen in a moderately moist climate, or one as nearly approaching the dry as can be endured without aggravating the cough. A permanent residence in a moist and hot climate is so enervating that it often leads to increased general debility.

For the most part the warm-moist and moderately moist climates are winter and spring resorts only, and are employed as palliatives to the disease while it is active and increasing. They insure to many a winter in the open air and under sunny skies. By avoiding the rigors of a Northern winter and spring, life is often prolonged, the disease is frequently checked, and time is gained in which a lasting improvement can be effected.

I have classed San Antonio among the moderately dry, warm climates, but it might almost equally well be grouped with the moderately moist, warm resorts. It is geographically on the border of both the warm-moist and warm-dry regions. In winter it is moderately dry, but during the remainder of the year it is moderately moist. The climate of Northern Georgia and South Carolina is, as regards humidity, very similar to that of the region about San Antonio, and is useful for the same class of cases. Thomasville, Georgia, and Asheville, South Carolina, are amid pine-forests. They are especially good in the fall, in the winter, and late spring, and the neighboring mountain resorts, in the summer, for just those cases that are benefited by moist, warm climates in winter. The influence of the balsamic air is peculiarly good for those who suffer from an irritative cough and copious expectoration. Most patients, for whom the warm, moist climate of Florida or the West Indies is best suited in winter, can pass comfortably and salubriously the late spring, summer, and early fall in Northern Georgia and South Carolina. Of resorts in the United States, those of Florida are types of the warm moist. I have already indicated the class of cases for which they are best adapted. Among the favorite resorts of this State are St. Augustine, Fernandina, and Cedar Keys upon the sea-coast, and Palatka in the interior. The sky is exceptionally clear and bright during the winter. The temperature is delightful to those who wish to escape the Northern cold. Upon the west coast of Florida the air is dry and similar to that of the coast of Southern California. Resorts along it may most properly be classed among those in dry, warm climates. Tarpon Springs is a comfortable and typical resort on this coast. It is attractive because of its climate, the luxuriance of vegetation, unsurpassed fishing and boating.

Foreign climates comparable to the Floridian are found at Madeira, Teneriffe, Cuba, Jamaica, the Bermudas, and the Sandwich Islands. In many of these places, and notably at Teneriffe, mountain altitudes may be combined with the equable, moist, warm climate. Tangiers, some of the Mediterranean isles, and points along the coast of Italy possess moderately moist, warm climates, but are not directly comparable to the interior climate of Georgia and South Carolina.

The balsamic forests at moderate elevations in the Adirondack Mountains are favorite summer resorts. They do not afford the advantages of a high altitude, but make possible mountain-climbing, hunting, fishing, boating, camping,—forms of exercise and modes of life that are most useful to those consumptives who possess strength to take advantage of them.

Ocean voyages have long been famous for their good influence upon consumption. But what is true of land climates is true of the ocean-air: it is not equally well adapted to every case. In discussing land climates, I have enumerated several sea-shore and island resorts. These combine the elements of the land and ocean climate. The influence of the ocean climate in its purity is only obtainable on a vessel at sea. On so chronic a disease as consumption, it exerts little influence except when the voyage is a prolonged one. The characteristic element of the ocean climate is the purity of its air. In mid-ocean the air is almost absolutely free from dust; therefore, from noxious germs. It is rich in the most energetic and useful form of oxygen. It is chiefly this quality that makes the ocean climate a tonic one to the digestive organs, and causes it to promote better general nutrition. The temperature is peculiarly equable. There is at sea less difference between winter and summer temperature and night and day temperature than upon land. By day the water absorbs much heat, as the sun's rays penetrate it deeply. It gives off less heat than land, for much water is transformed into vapor by the heat, which is thus made latent. Moreover, the vapor upon the water limits the radiation of heat from it by night. In winter the cool air is warmed by the slow radiation of heat from the deeply-heated ocean. The surface water is cooled, at once sinks and is replaced by warmer. This process continues until the heat absorbed deeply by day and in summer has been given off. An ocean climate is always a moist one. The variation in its humidity is very slight. A sea-air also contains a minute amount of chlorine, iodine, and bromine, which may have some effect upon animal life.

A sea-air is usually sedative in its action upon the nervous system, and promotes sleep. Complete isolation from all affairs of the world guarantees to one taking an ocean voyage a mental rest and relief from business strain. This is important in many cases of incipient consumption. Overmental exertion is frequently a characteristic of the consumptive. The ocean air lessens, as a rule, irritative, harsh coughing. Its moisture makes expectoration and breathing easier. The appetite with as much uniformity is improved. Nourishment is better appropriated by the tissues, and therefore flesh and strength increase.

Long voyages are particularly beneficial to those who are predisposed to the disease, especially if the lungs are reasonably well developed; to those who are scrofulous; to those who suffer from frequent hæmorrhages, which are often checked by the sea-air; to those with a moderate degree of consolidation and contraction of the lungs and a harsh, irritating, and wearying cough. Those who are very weak, and in whom much improvement cannot be expected, should not make such trips, for they cannot turn back if they grow worse. Those who have much fever should not venture to sea for the same reason. There are those who suffer from sea-sickness continuously while on the water, and for such a voyage would be harmful, and would of necessity lead to greater bodily wasting. Persons are rarely met who are so timid while at sea that their constant apprehension depresses them and prevents their experiencing the benefits which otherwise they might. For them, also, sea-voyages are useless, if not hurtful. Another drawback to the successful treatment of consumptives at sea is the limited number of exercises that can be taken. This is a drawback which men rarely feel unless they are upon a crowded steamer, for, besides promenading and the usual deck-games, they can help the sailors or take varied gymnastic exercises in the rigging. A voyage on a sailing vessel, I believe, is much to be preferred to one on a steamer. Prolonged stormy weather is detrimental to the successful treatment of lung disease, for it usually compels passengers to remain in close and poorly ventilated cabins for hours, and sometimes days, continuously.

Voyages, to accomplish much good, should be of several weeks' and often better of several months' duration. A direction and season should be chosen that will be most likely to insure pleasant weather. It is usually desirable to get those for whom sea-voyages are adapted away from winter's cold and frequent changes of temperature. We can insure them two years of continuous summer by having them sail from the northern temperate zone to the southern, starting in October or November and returning in the spring.

The shorter ocean voyages are to the West Indies, Azores, or a Spanish or Mediterranean port by slow steamer or good ship. The longer ones are to South American ports or to Cape of Good Hope, or to Australia or India by the Pacific.

Results as beneficial as have been obtained at high altitudes have been obtained at sea. Both insure pure air and make possible out-door life.

They stimulate to exercise and the tissues of the body to greater nutritive activity.

In choosing a climate for individual cases, other things than the effect of it upon the lungs must be thought of. Especially for those who are weak and whose appetites are capricious a place must be chosen where good, wholesome, varied, and well-cooked food can be had. In choosing between similar climates in our own and foreign countries the taste of individuals must be considered. For those who are moderately strong and naturally fond of sports and active exercise, there is little trouble in making a selection. But for those habituated to a sedentary life, and naturally disposed to take little exercise, a location must be chosen whose natural features are so attractive and varied that they will awaken interest and lead to exercise, or else a resort must be selected where a medical man is located who will guide and stimulate those who need it to the necessary degree of activity.

The condition of the digestive organs or nervous system may make unsuitable to a given individual a climate that would be perfectly adapted to the condition of his lungs. There is still a larger class of cases who must have an occupation by which they can support themselves wherever they go. For such, frequent and especially seasonal changes are impossible, and a permanent residence must be chosen where work can be found. It is, therefore, evident that often a choice of climate is no easy matter.

The selection of a climate is frequently made easier by watching the effect, in a given patient, of different kinds of weather, especially of bright, warm, moist days, and bright, warm, dry ones.

There are, unfortunately, many cases for whom no climatic changes are desirable. All cases of quick consumption should be advised to remain at home, for a change is useless. Cases of tubercular disease of the larynx are little benefited by climatic changes. Those who have continuous fever are usually best off at home. An exception to the last rule I would make for those who are fairly strong and not losing ground rapidly, and who, by a change, can be sure of enjoying continuous out-door life. If cavities are enlarging rapidly, or extreme weakness prevents exercise, a change is of no use. Discomfort and no benefit is produced by changes that are made when life is fast ebbing or nearly ended.

There are many consumptives who, for financial or other reasons, cannot seek the climates best adapted to their conditions. Hope need not be lost because of this. We see recoveries occurring here in Chicago in those who are predisposed to the disease, and who suffer in its earlier stages. The chances of successful treatment are, however, much less in any other than the climate best adapted to each case. Unfortunately, our most populous cities and States are located in a changeable, cool, damp climate, which especially excites or aggravates inflammation in the respiratory tracts.

These are locations illy suited to the treatment of consumption. If a change cannot be made, care in the execution of the other rules of life essential to the treatment of consumption must be redoubled.

CHAPTER VII.

Hygiene (*continued*).

EXERCISE.

The importance of exercise and the desirability of its being taken out-of-doors have already been frequently adverted to. Exercise must be adapted to the stage of the disease and to the peculiarities of muscular development in each individual. It must be general; that is, must call into play most of the muscles of the body. It must also be special, or addressed to the development of those muscles that may be peculiarly weak or small.

General exercise, such as is taken in brisk walking, running, and horseback-riding, or, better, in these combined with others, for the arms and chest-muscles promote better nutrition. This is accomplished by invigorating the circulation, and especially the lymph circulation. It is by the latter that nutriment is brought in direct contact with the elements of the tissues, and by it waste products are removed. The successive contraction and extension of muscles is one of the most important factors in the maintenance of vigorous circulation of the lymph. It promotes restful sleep by causing a healthy weariness. Regular exercise out-of-doors will often lessen or check night-sweats in those who are a little feverish. Such sweats are, without doubt, due to the presence of some deleterious substance produced in the body by the abnormal action of the diseased tissues. In some instances it can apparently be destroyed or eliminated. Its elimination is undoubtedly aided by exercise. We often observe the rise of fever and return of night-sweats in those who, by inclement weather, have been housed for a few days, and we observe their diminution or disappearance when again the accustomed open-air exercise is resumed. However, the most important and most constant result of exercise is the promotion of better nutrition.

Active—that is, voluntary—exercise is always to be preferred. Indeed, it is rare that voluntary exercise cannot be taken by the consumptive, unless he is too feeble to bear any. Massage, which is the form of involuntary or passive exercise most frequently resorted to, is, therefore, rarely useful in consumption. It may be employed for those who are well able, but too lazy or sluggish, for active exertion.

The amount of exercise should be adapted to the strength of the individual. It should never cause exhaustion, but may be carried to the point of producing gentle fatigue, which can be easily recovered from by a little rest. It accomplishes the most good when it is distributed over the day in small amounts. It should be varied; for of exercise, as of food or books, one tires, if it is unvaried in character.

Among the best and most easily utilized forms of exercise are walking, running, climbing, riding, bicycling, tennis, and other sports. Walking to be useful must be brisk, and the arms must be permitted to swing freely at the side. Nothing lessens the good effects of walking so much as persistently holding the arms at the sides, with the hands in pockets or a muff. These positions interfere with exercise of the muscles of the shoulders, and with free, deep breathing. Walking chiefly exercises the legs. Those predisposed to consumption, or suffering from its more chronic forms, with thoracic contraction, should above all be urged to exercise the arms and to breath deeply. Hill-climbing, especially if the climber carries an Alpine stick or long staff, is peculiarly good, for it enforces deeper breathing than level walking does. The lifting forward with each step of a staff that is grasped at a point nearly as high as one's shoulder enforces a lifting of the arm and straightening of the shoulders which is mild but excellent exercise for the arms and chest. Running is a general exercise, but also an especially good exercise for the muscles of respiration, as it necessitates frequent and deep breathing. Rowing is especially useful in strengthening the muscles of the arms, shoulders, respiration, and less vigorously those of other parts of the body. Horseback-riding and bicycling produce a gentle general exercise. Rapid bicycling, or wheeling over heavy ground, causes the rider to lean forward so that respiration is rather impeded than aided. It is not, under such conditions, a useful exercise. Field sports and gunning are excellent forms of exercise, and are exhilarating for those who are strong enough to bear them. They are almost exclusively adapted to those who are predisposed but not yet affected by consumption. The necessity of never carrying exercise to the point of exhaustion must be borne in mind.

Those whose chests are abnormally small in circumference, or who are round-shouldered or otherwise deformed through lack of muscular vigor, can accomplish much by exercises especially adapted to meet their peculiar needs, that can be taken in any well-appointed gymnasium. Gymnasium exercise should never be practiced to the exclusion of out-door exercise. I have already dwelt on the need of special training, which will ultimately lead to a symmetrical development of the body, for those in the earlier years of life, predisposed to consumption. Similar, but, at first, more gentle exercise is needed by those in whom the disease has caused flattening of the chest. Violent or prolonged exercise should be avoided by all who are much feverish. This, however, is a general rule, for occasionally a consumptive is found who has a daily and considerable rise of temperature, who is comparatively vigorous and energetic. Those who are feverish should be permitted only gently fatiguing exercise. We cannot gauge the amount of exercise that should be taken, either by the degree of bodily heat or lack of energy, but only by the strength of the individual. There are many who are languid and disinclined to physical exertion, who are both able to take it and sure of benefit from it.

If possible, all exercise should be taken out-of-doors. During rainy weather, if the sun appears between the clouds, advantage should be taken of the few minutes of brightness for a walk and a breath of fresh air.

In our latitude exercise is best taken, during the summer months, in the first hours of the forenoon or last ones of the afternoon. In late autumn, winter, and early spring, it should be taken near midday. All consumptives should pass as much of the day out-of-doors as their strength will permit them to do. If the climate they are in will allow it, they should rest in the open air as well as exercise there so long as it is daylight.

Of the special exercises the most important are those that expand and enlarge the chest and insure thorough ventilation of the lungs with clean air. But often other deformities than that of a narrow or shrunken chest, such as rounded shoulders and stooped neck, must be corrected. For the modification of many of these, the instructions of a physician and of a gymnasium's director must be relied upon. In order to correct the condition of stooped neck and rounded shoulders, the first requisite is the removal of the causes. Leaning over a book or desk or sewing-machine, or sitting upon a shoe-maker's or tailor's bench, or for other reasons maintaining for hours continuously a stooping posture, is the commonest cause. Such a posture prevents the free and frequent use of the muscles that maintain a straight, erect position, and from disuse they waste and are weakened. No occupation necessitating the maintenance of such positions should be chosen by those who have consumption or are predisposed to it. If they must be followed, the habit should be acquired of straightening the back, neck, and shoulders, and deeply filling the chest as often as every half or three-quarters of an hour. If the head droops forward habitually, crooking the neck, it is impossible easily to fill the lungs, and if the shoulders round forward the upper part of the lungs cannot be expanded completely. Consumption almost invariably begins in the top of the lungs, because, as is supposed, the air is less easily and perfectly changed there. The need of perfect expansion of this part of the lungs of those predisposed to the disease is self-evident. Originating at the top of the lungs, it tends to contract and cripple this part of them; therefore, forcible expansion is necessary to counteract the tendency. An erect carriage should be striven for by all who are predisposed to the malady, or have it.

There are special exercises, and even special forms of apparatus in gymnasiums, for the correction of these deformities, but to describe them is outside the province of this essay. A few general directions may be of value. While sitting or standing, an erect position should always be maintained. While walking, the head should be held up, the neck kept straight, and the shoulders thrown back. The top of the lungs will be inflated most surely if the muscles down the front of the abdomen are slightly contracted while an inspiration is taken. Indeed, strong and firm abdominal muscles are essential to good breathing. The habit of standing and walking erect is best acquired by permitting the eyes to wander among objects about fifteen or twenty feet above the ground and fifty or one hundred feet away. The reading of signs above store windows and doors is often a useful amusement. The muscles of the neck are well exercised by balancing a book or other light object upon the head while sitting or walking. However, if one will remember to hold the head erect, there is rarely sufficient loss of muscular strength to make it difficult. The same we may say of straightening the shoulders. Indeed, if one will constantly endeavor to hold the head up, the shoulders back, the back straight, and the abdomen flat, the muscles of all these parts will be sufficiently exercised to keep them strong and vigorous. In those, however, who inherit a predisposition to consumption, or already have the disease, and especially if it is in its chronic form, the muscles about the shoulders are shrunken and weak. Not only must they be strengthened to acquire a symmetrical muscular development over the body, but to hold the shoulders back, and, as they are employed in deep breathing, to aid it. In general, we may say that pulling and pushing from the shoulders call these muscles into use and strengthen them. Rowing is, therefore, beneficial. To accomplish the most good, the pushing and pulling should be varied, and from different directions. Dumb-bell exercises help to strengthen the muscles of the shoulders and arms. Calisthenics, without dumb-bells, are often sufficient. An especially good exercise consists in swinging the extended arms backward as far as possible, keeping them, at the same time, in a horizontal position. One may stand in a door-way, and, grasping its sides, permit the body to lean backward at arms' length, and then pull it forward into the erect position. In this way, the pulling muscles of the arms and shoulders are used, one's own body being the object pulled. The pushing muscles may be exercised by standing back from the door-way and, leaning the hands against its sides, permit the body to lean forward as far as possible, and then push it back into an upright position. To develop the muscles best, pushing and pulling should not be forward and backward only, but sideways and upward and downward also. Each exercise should be persevered in until it produces gentle fatigue. The exerciser should endeavor every day to repeat the motions oftener, and with increased rapidity. If this can be done without increasing the degree of weariness, the muscles are surely growing stronger.

In order to expand to normal proportions a chest contracted from imperfect development or from disease, nothing is so important as respiratory gymnastics proper. By respiratory gymnastics proper, I mean enforced and frequent deep and slow inspiration and expiration. The necessity for such exercises cannot be too greatly emphasized. They are needful always when a predisposition to consumption exists; also, when the disease is causing a slow contraction and deformity of the thorax. They often aid in loosening and expelling tenacious mucus from the bronchial tubes.

Deep breathing causes better oxygenation of the blood, and thus stimulates a better degree of nutrition in all the tissues. Not only does frequent deep breathing supply more oxygen to the blood, but it removes from it more perfectly carbonic acid and water, which is to be exhaled. Deep inspiration causes the blood-vessels of the lungs to fill, and withdraws as much from the veins elsewhere in the body; prolonged expiration, on the other hand, presses the blood from the vessels of the lungs and permits the systemic veins to become distended. These circulatory changes in the lungs are useful to the consumptive, insuring a better oxygenation of a larger volume of blood and giving the vessels greater strength by training them to readily contract and expand. The more palpable effects are enlargement of the lungs and strengthening of the respiratory muscles.

Those who are predisposed to consumption or suffering from the disease in its earlier stages should adhere to the rule of drawing slowly as deep an inspiration as possible, as often as every three to five minutes while walking out-of-doors, and as often as every half-hour while sitting in-doors. When an inspiration is taken, the head should be erect so that the neck, and therefore the wind-pipe, will be straight, and will readily transmit air; the shoulders should be thrown back so that the upper part of the chest can be fully inflated; and the inspiration should be made through the nose with the mouth closed. By such inspirations, all the respiratory muscles are exercised and made to grow strong; the air-cavities of the lungs are filled or distended; and the whole chest is gradually enlarged, especially in its lateral and transverse diameters. Furthermore, frequent, enforced deep breathing leads to its habitual practice. There is not a more important habit for the consumptive to acquire. Hill-climbing causes involuntary deep breathing. Running, for the same reason, is an invaluable exercise. It is particularly useful to enlarge the lungs. I frequently advise consumptives, in the early stages of the disease, to practice running daily. This cannot be well done by daylight in a crowded city, but advantage should be taken of each clear night. Each day a little greater distance should be run, and gradually a little quicker gait should be acquired.

The effect of slow inspiration can be increased by breathing through one nostril only. Coincident deep inspiration and prolonged expiration are desirable. Deep inspiration necessitates a somewhat prolonged expiration. The latter can sometimes be advantageously further prolonged by closing one nostril or by producing certain sounds which necessitate various degrees of closure of the throat by the vocal chords. Deep inspiration causes a fall of air-pressure in the lungs, and prolonged expiration causes increased air-pressure. Practically, therefore, unusually deep breathing produces the effect of breathing in a condensed air, since, as compared with that in the lungs, the atmospheric air is condensed; and prolonged expiration produces the effect of exhaling into a rarefied air, as that within the lungs is compressed. This compression can be increased by closing both mouth and nostrils at the end of deep inspiration, and making an expulsive effort. Such compression of the air in the lungs forces open all the air-spaces within the chest, and decidedly promotes the absorption of inflammatory exudates and the loosening of secretions within the bronchial tubes. The effects are the same as that which, to an increased degree, can be obtained from the inhalation of air artificially compressed and exhalation into air similarly rarefied.

Breathing exercises would not be so necessary if all the air the lungs contain was changed with each respiration, but this is not the case. While each lung ordinarily contains about two hundred and twenty cubic inches of air, twenty only are breathed in and out with each quiet respiratory movement. If an unusually long inspiration is made, one hundred and ten cubic inches can be added to what each lung contains, and if an unusually complete expiration is made after such an inspiration two hundred and thirty cubic inches can be forced out. It is evident, therefore, that, ordinarily, one-third the actual capacity of the lungs is unused. If irritants gain lodgment in these unused portions, they are likely to remain long enough to do irreparable harm; but it is scarcely possible for foreign substances to remain in those portions constantly emptied and filled. This is one reason why it is desirable that the entire lung-capacity should be brought into use. Moreover, in those parts of the lungs where there is air, but where it is rarely or slowly changed, waste matter that should be exhaled accumulates, and if disease exists in or near these areas products of its action may be formed, and be re-absorbed, and prove poisonous to the body. It has often been experimentally proven that the exhalations from healthy lungs are poisonous. If slowly and continuously absorbed, they cause languor, loss of appetite, and loss of mental as well as physical vigor. But enforced deep breathing insures perfect ventilation of all parts of the lungs, and, as is almost self-evident, helps to prevent infection when contaminated air is breathed, and also to eliminate deleterious materials generated by the human system both in health and disease. It is evident that the ill effects of imperfect ventilation are most apt to be developed in those whose lung-capacity has been greatly diminished by the acquirement of rounded or stooped shoulders or other deforming attitudes, or by disease which destroys the air-space.

I have seen the circumference of the chest increased two inches in six months by deep breathing and complete expiration, practiced very frequently for an hour in the morning and again for an hour in the evening. At the same time, the amount of air exhaled during quiet breathing was increased very appreciably, and all respiratory movements were made more forceful. This increased forcefulness is important, since it insures the deep stirring of the air in the lungs. The invigoration which these exercises wrought, together with good food and air, transformed in nine months a listless and half-invalid stripling, six feet in height, weighing 135 pounds, with narrow and long chest, into a vigorous youth, with broadened shoulders, whose weight was 180 pounds.

What may at first be an enforced or voluntary deep and complete respiration becomes by frequent and persistent repetition a habit and involuntary. It is this habit that should be striven for. One's general physical vigor, as well as the healthfulness of one's lungs, largely depends upon their perfect ventilation, and, therefore, upon the thorough oxygenation of the blood and its purification. But deep and especially very deep breathing produces other mechanical effects which have been described, and which are useful and absolutely necessary to many consumptives, but may be even harmful to others. There can be gotten from enforced deep breathing nearly the same results as from breathing the air of high altitudes. The results are attained more slowly, and require more of voluntary effort and constant thoughtfulness on the part of the one seeking them. Therefore, to those for whom a high-altitude climate is desirable, but for any reason unattainable, these respiratory gymnastics are all important. They must be largely relied upon to develop the crippled lungs, to remove foreign, waste, and deleterious matters by ventilation, and to invigorate the whole system by the addition of needed oxygen.

Enforced respiratory exercises should not be employed during or immediately after hæmorrhages from the lungs, as they may prolong or renew the bleeding by preventing the blood-clots from plugging the bleeding vessel or by loosening them from it. They should not be employed when there is much fever, and in a very gentle and moderate way when a slight increase of temperature exists. Very great debility makes their employment impossible, and often, if attempted, causes such weariness as to be harmful. If large cavities exist, they also contra-indicate much respiratory exercise.

Respiratory exercises are especially useful when the elasticity of the lungs has been lessened by disuse or disease, and the amount of air habitually exhaled and inhaled is too small; when the chest is narrow, thin, or deformed; and when catarrhal inflammation exists, and it is desirable to loosen and expel secretions from the bronchial tubes. The best results are attainable in the earlier years of life; that is, during youth and early manhood, when the bony frame-work of the chest is still pliable, and the upbuilding power of the tissues is great. When exercises are prescribed for consumptives, they must be adapted to the stage of advancement of the disease and its degree of acuteness. The same exercises are adapted to those who are predisposed to it and those suffering from its incipient results. Those in the earlier years of life, in whom the disease is farther advanced, though for the time quiescent, must take the same classes of exercise, but with much greater moderation; especially must they be careful not to produce considerable exhaustion. Individuals belonging to these classes must aim to correct deformities and imperfect muscular development by special exercise, to enlarge the lungs by either voluntary or involuntary pulmonary gymnastics, and to thus effect a general invigoration. Running, brisk and prolonged walks, mountain-climbing, riding, and boating, out-of-door sports, as ball and tennis, or hunting and fishing, are the most useful and promptly effective forms of exercise or combined sports. If business is carried on while treatment is being pursued, the hours for exercise and the kind taken must be fully prescribed and efficiently superintended. As these exercises must be persevered in for long periods of time, they must occasionally be varied, that they may not become too irksome. Interest in them can be maintained by periodically taking measurements of the chest when fully expanded and completely emptied, and noting the difference as increased chest capacity and mobility are acquired, and by testing the strength of various sets of muscles as they are being developed, and by observing the degrees of endurance which are attained. With all these exercises, it is best to combine systematic and enforced deep breathing.

To those who have a nightly access of fever, but a normal temperature during the greater part of the day, and who are able to be dressed, and even to do considerable walking, a life out-of-doors is still possible. Carriage-riding will afford pleasure and gentle exercise. Short and frequent walks can be taken. Deep breathing can also be practiced, but less frequently and systematically than when no fever exists. Often deep inhalation provokes coughing or pain, and cannot, for these reasons, be made.

If fever is continuous throughout the day, several hours can be spent in the open air in a hammock, or in a seat by the open window, and an occasional drive can be taken, or, perhaps, a few moments' walk before the door. More exercise usually is impossible, or causes harmful exhaustion. Those who are forty years old or more, in whom the disease is in its incipiency, or is quiescent, can take much more exercise in quantity than those with slight fever, but it must be for the most part the same in character. Its object must be to insure complete ventilation of the lungs and as complete use of them as possible; but there is little hope of correcting deformities and compensating for lung destruction.

Those who are bedridden are unable to take exercise, and are usually harmed if they try it.

CHAPTER VIII.

Hygiene (*continued*).

CLOTHING.

I HAVE already explained the need of keeping the bodies of those who are predisposed to consumption completely protected against atmospheric changes by woolen clothing. Such protection is just as needful for those in whom the disease is established or advanced. Wool is preferable, for it maintains a very equitable temperature about the body; it is light and porous, and is not expensive. It should be worn both by night and day. Its weight should be varied with the seasons. It is an error to think that to increase warmth clothing must be heavy. It should be light, in no way cumbersome, and sufficiently porous to allow of the exit of bodily exhalations. Not unfrequently we see persons who have disease of the lungs who are over-clothed, wearing, it may be, two sets of underwear, a chest-protector, a knitted garment inside the dress, a small shawl pinned closely round the bust, and then a large, heavy shawl over the shoulders. Such dressing is not conducive to cleanliness, for several of the elements of the costume are rarely taken off, and are never well aired or washed. It is not conducive to health, as the weight of the costume is burdensome. So many wraps prevent the ready removal of exhalations from the skin and the easy expansion of the chest.

Chest-protectors may be beneficial or harmful. If made of woolen cloth, and not too thick, they are serviceable, but if they are made of leather they cannot be healthful, for they prevent the absorption of exhalations and secretions from the skin and their removal to the outside air. The skin is an important adjunct of the lungs and kidneys in removing from the body waste and deleterious products of life. If the skin is covered by impervious clothing, its eliminative functions are interfered with. Every tissue and organ in the consumptive must be given the best chance to do its work, or must be aided, certainly not hindred. For the same reason it is not well, for any great length of time, to wear leather or waterproof garments.

Clothing should always be loose, and in no

way impede respiration. Corsets and tight belts should not be worn. Especially are they harmful during the years of growth, when the chest is being molded. They greatly interfere with abdominal respiration, which is essential to perfect filling of the chest.

Health should never be endangered for fashion's sake. The exposure of necks and arms to the drafts of ball-rooms, and to sudden chilling because of imperfect protection by wraps when hot and close rooms are left, especially during winter and other inclement seasons, is a source of great and unnecessary danger.

Mufflers are wrapped about the face and are held over the mouth and nose by many persons in cold weather. This is a detrimental habit, unless one is walking or riding against a severe wind or forced to breath a damp and cold air. Dry, cold air should not be feared; and it must be remembered that of all things pure air and unhindered breathing is what is most essential for those whose lungs are crippled. Heavy veils and mufflers are often temporarily useful when a sudden transition from a warm air to a cold one provokes severe coughing. But even when worn for this reason, they should be gradually removed after the transition is made, and should be employed in order that the transition can be gradually made.

DIET.

A gain in flesh by consumptives is accompanied by a gain in strength, a diminution of cough, and greater feeling of well-being. It is, therefore, necessary at all times to strive not only to stop waste, but to promote gain in flesh. The natural tendency of consumption is to cause gradual, steady bodily waste. Therefore, this tendency must be combated by the administration of food, and by aiding when necessary its digestion and assimilation. Whenever the disease is progressing in its destructive course, it is accompanied by fever. This fact must be borne in mind, and the influence of a fever upon digestion and assimilation considered. Moreover, the consumptive often has no appetite for food, and sometimes even a disinclination for it. This, also, is a condition that must be combated. In a much smaller number of cases there exists inflammation of the stomach, which interferes with digestion, and therefore increases the rapidity of bodily waste. Fortunately, these latter cases are comparatively few. Their diet and treatment depend upon the character of the disease of the stomach. It is not pertinent to the subject of this essay to consider the diet of those whose stomachs are inflamed. The larger number of individuals who lack appetite have no trouble in digesting what they do take. Their disinclination arises from nervous influences. Often a change of scene will remove this apathy, and they will at once eat well, or a succession of bright and cheerful days will cause improvement of appetite, and clouds and storms will again destroy it. To such individuals food in considerable quantities has been forcibly administered in spite of their disinclination, and it was uniformly digested easily, and caused a gain in flesh. The ingenuity and patience of the physician is sorely taxed in suggesting tempting foods or modes of administering them.

Change of scene and food is oftenest relied upon to improve the appetite, and when this mode of treatment cannot be used attempts to maintain nutrition are too frequently discontinued. Forced feeding and a gain in flesh will often bend the inclinations and cause a return of appetite. In health we can largely trust our appetite to dictate what and how much we shall eat, but in ill health this is impossible, and eating must be done not to satisfy desire, but to maintain life or strength. Food has been administered to consumptives, disinclined to eat, through a stomach-tube, in prescribed quantities. Their flesh and strength increased. The method of feeding is, however, so distasteful to most that, although it effects good results, it is rarely employed. More frequently food is taken with regularity as to time, quantity, and kind, by the physician's prescription, and without reference to the individual's desire. In this way forced feeding is maintained. Food containing nourishment in the most concentrated form is to be preferred. It must also be easily digestible and assimilable. Moreover, it is best given in small amounts, often; for instance, one or two wineglassfuls of milk every hour or two. Thus, in twenty-four hours the needful quantity is administered, but in amounts at a time so small as not to be noticeable or to create distress. The best foods at these times are milk, eggs, gruels, supplemented by cream or butter, or codliver-oil. The latter must be administered with especial care, so that its taking does not prove disgusting.

From earliest times milk has been regarded as peculiarly serviceable in restoring flesh and strength to the consumptive. It is easily taken. It contains, in almost perfect proportion, all the ingredients needed to maintain life. It is readily digested and appropriated by the human system. Under all circumstances milk should constitute a very prominent element of the consumptive's diet. If the invalid has some appetite, but one that is capricious, it should be pampered at meal-times by varied, appetizing dishes; but at other times, as a part of routine treatment, a glass of milk should be taken. How many of these should be drunk will depend on how much of other kinds of food is taken. A milk cure or an exclusively milk diet has been popular at different times, and in many countries. These cures consist in an exclusive milk-diet for many weeks, and often months. Sanitaria for those who wish to try it have been established. Good results have certainly been obtained, but it is not a mode of treatment adapted to all cases.

Soft-cooked and raw eggs are excellent nutriment, but, though strength-giving, they are not as flesh-producing as are oily and vegetable products. In consumption it is especially flesh-production that should be stimulated.

A vegetable diet which supplies an abundance

of starch and sugar is more flesh-producing than an albuminous one. But neither a purely albuminous or vegetable diet is the best. For those who have little or no daily fever, an abundance of sugars, starches, and oils are the best; but, if fever is quite constant and high, a larger proportion of albumen usually proves most serviceable. Those consumptives whose appetites and digestion are good should use the same mixed diet that one in health would use.

Malt extracts are often prescribed for consumptives. In the market are two kinds,—one comparatively thin and in reality a very sweet beer; the second, a thick syrup without alcohol. The first, as an article of diet, must be classed with the alcoholics. The second consists of sugar and a digestive agent, which acts as does the saliva and pancreatic juice upon starch, converting it into sugar. Therefore, these extracts are both food and aids to digestion. They are useful, but especially when there is no fever, or a very slight or irregular fever. They will not replace other foods, but are useful in adding to the regimen a needed excess of carbohydrates, and in aiding their digestion.

The circumstances that make starches and

sugars useful make oils so. All oils are of advantage to consumptives, but they are not all digested with equal ease. It is well, for those who can take them without discomfort, to use, freely, butter, cream, and table-oils. The varied desserts and fruits upon which cream can be used are, therefore, peculiarly good. Oatmeal and cracked wheat, rice, and other similar dishes, are made more nutritious by the use of cream upon them. For the same reason bacon is useful and easily digestible, if fried hard. Of all the oils, that which is most famous as an aid to the consumptive is codliver-oil. Unfortunately, this is so distasteful to many that it cannot always be given in sufficiently large doses to accomplish much good. Its field of usefulness is much increased since various palatable preparations of it have been devised. It is peculiarly serviceable because it is so readily absorbed from the stomach and intestines. The readiness with which it is absorbed is probably partly due to an admixture with it of some bile from the cod-liver. It is also more than a food, as it contains minute quantities of iodine, bromine, phosphorus, and other ingredients which act in part medicinally. That great benefit can be derived from its use cannot be doubted, but it must be given in suitable cases if these results are wished for. If the stomach is inflamed, it should not be given. If there is constant and high fever, it does no good. It must not be given in larger amounts than are easily digested. If it eructates into the mouth for hours after it is taken, it is evident that it is not being well digested, or has been taken in too large quantities; and usually, under such circumstances, it destroys the appetite for other food. Then it does harm. Neither should the oils be given in amounts larger than are readily borne by the stomach, nor simultaneously with large quantities of cream and fats, lest the fat-digesting power of the intestines be overtaxed, and they cause irritation and a detrimental indigestion. It is most useful in the most chronic cases, and when the disease is least active. It then increases flesh, prompts a better appetite, lessens cough, and renders the sputa less matter- or pus- like. All the bodily functions seem to be invigorated by it. Certainly codliver-oil should be tried by all consumptives in whom a fever or indigestion does not contra-indicate it.

The clear, light-colored oils are the best. The brown and strong-smelling oils are not so easily digested or so wholesome. Codliver-oil should be taken during or immediately after meals. The amount which can be taken varies greatly with individuals. As a rule, its use should be begun by the administration of a half-teaspoonful twice daily. The dose should be gradually increased to as large an amount as is well borne. It is rare that more than a tablespoonful can be taken three times daily, and in the larger proportion of cases not more than a teaspoonful three times daily can be used. Children will sooner learn to use the oil without distaste and in proportionately larger doses than adults. It is best given as clear oil when it can be thus taken. Often a pinch of salt taken before and after the oil rapidly removes from the mouth the unpleasant fish-taste. It can also be easily taken by many in ice-water. So much ice-cold water should be placed in a glass as can be taken in one swallow, and to this the oil should be added. The oil will gather in a mass in the centre of the water, and if the whole is swallowed at once it will be scarcely tasted. By others it is more easily taken if a little of any bitter tonic, like the tincture of gentian or nux vomica, is added to it. Many emulsions of the oil are sold and are very palatable. They constitute, for many patients, the most agreeable mode of administering it. It must be remembered that not more than half of their bulk consists of oil. The oil is also sold in soft, elastic capsules, and when thus taken is tasteless. Capsules are made which contain from 10 drops to a tablespoonful of oil. The latter are so large as to appear formidable, but are swallowed with ease by many persons. Capsules containing from 20 to 60 drops are readily swallowed. To take an ordinary dose, from two to six of the smaller capsules must be taken at a time.

Alcoholics are regarded by so many as strength-giving, and are so often resorted to by consumptives, that it seems best to explain their exact mode of action and the results of experience in their use. The alcohol in all beverages containing it acts the same, but occurs in very different amounts in different ones. The other ingredients of these beverages have some varying effect.

If alcohol is added to a dish of food that is being artificially digested by a chemist with gastric or pancreatic juice, it will retard that digestion in proportion to the amount added. When, however, alcoholic beverages are taken into the human stomach, they do not always act thus. If the stomach is inflamed they will irritate it, aggravate the inflammation, and decidedly retard digestion. If they are taken into a healthy stomach in diluted form they mildly irritate it, causing it to form a somewhat increased amount of acid in the gastric juice. This may hasten digestion, or, if the stomach is empty, cause warmth in it, which amounts in some cases to heart-burn. If these dilute doses are often repeated, and especially if large amounts, or beverages containing large proportions, of alcohol are taken, the stomach becomes constantly irritated, then mildly and by degrees chronically inflamed. That these beverages should never be used in inflamed conditions of the stomach need hardly be said.

Unfortunately, alcoholics do not affect the digestive organs only. When absorbed and taken into the blood, alcohol at once so affects it that it cannot take up from the air in the lungs as large a proportion of oxygen as is natural. This necessarily lessens the rapidity of tissue-changes. It diminishes perfect oxidation of worn-out tissues which should be oxidized and eliminated, and leads to the retention of some product that should be gotten rid of. If by the habitual use of these beverages the blood is kept constantly from performing its whole work, there are gradually produced degenerative changes in the tissues. The rapidity with which these are produced will vary with the amount of alcohol constantly used, and with the susceptibility of the individual to its influence. It must be remembered that the destruction of lung-tissue, which consumption causes of itself, diminishes the amount of oxygen which can be appropriated by the blood for its use. Alcoholics continuously given, therefore, only heighten the deleterious effect of the disease. But not only is tissue-change which involves the natural elimination of used-up matter interfered with, but the capability of the tissues to take up new matter is also lessened. The considerable diminution of tissue-change which large doses of alcohol will produce causes a lowering of temperature which is quite perceptible in fever. Fever of itself is always accompanied by and possibly caused by imperfect and abnormal chemical changes in the tissues. The products of these imperfect changes are in themselves often poisonous, and produce the languid feelings and mental dullness which so uniformly accompanies fever. Under these circumstances it is certainly not advisable to give alcoholics, which add another disturbing and deleterious influence. They lower the temperature, but do not therefore remove the cause of the fever or stop its ravages. They only change its aspect. We can say, then, that alcoholics should not be given continuously, as they impair the normal activity of the blood, and certainly not when consumptives are feverish.

Alcoholics also influence the heart and blood-vessels. Small amounts given to those not habituated to them cause a quicker heart's action for a few minutes. If given steadily, the blood-vessels dilate and the pressure within them is lessened. By large doses the heart's action is weakened.

Cough is lessened if these beverages are given continuously or in moderately large amounts. The anæsthetic properties of alcohol accomplish this. It dulls the sensibilities and lessens cough, just as small doses of opiates do. It lessens the power of appreciating discomfort, and thus produces a feeling of false well-being.

I feel convinced, from theoretic considerations, as well as from observation of tests, that alcohol is not a food. Alcoholic beverages contain no other elements that can act as food than sugar, which exists in some of them in small quantities. It is hardly necessary, however, to take these beverages in order to get the small amount of sugar which they contain.

The views of medical men have changed much within a few years in regard to the use of these beverages in consumption and other diseases. This change has been wrought by a better knowledge of their mode of action, and by trials, even to the excessive use, of them. Statistics have been gathered which show that those consumptives who use liquors live, on an average, some months less than those who do not.

Cleanliness is always a necessity if health is to be maintained. It is unnecessary to comment upon this requirement.

Mental excess, anxiety, sorrow, and misfortune which depresses often hasten the development of the disease or make its progress ungovernable, for they lessen physical vitality. Therefore, these conditions should be avoided or counteracted when they threaten or exist. Change of scene is the most potent means we know of for diverting the mind.

On the other hand, pleasures and recreations

which lead to lightness of heart and good temper are to be cultivated. A search for such as will prove best suited to individuals is frequently a trying but important task for the physician.

Abstinence from excesses and intemperance of passions is also essential.

CHAPTER IX.

MEDICINAL TREATMENT AND POSSIBILITIES OF CURE.

As it is not my intention in this essay to consider the medicinal treatment of consumption, it is not necessary to discuss separate symptoms of the disease. There are, however, two or three that are usually so distressing or alarming to the sufferers that it is best to refer to them. Of all the symptoms that accompany the disease, cough is the most constant. It is one of the first to attract attention, and is often so severe as to be distressing and wearisome. I refer to this symptom not to recommend a treatment for it, but to call attention to the fact that frequently it should not be especially treated. Everything that gives the consumptive strength will enable him to bear the strain of coughing without weariness. Everything aimed to heal the lungs tends to remove the cough. So-called cough-medicines contain anodynes that allay cough by lessening the excitability of the nerves. The anodyne most used is morphine. This, when taken in efficient quantities, almost uniformly lessens the appetite, and often very considerably interferes with digestion. It tends to destroy what should especially be conserved,—digestion, flesh, and strength. Cough, when severe, must be treated; but frequently, even then, an anodyne need be administered not more than once or twice daily. By preference it should be given at bed-time, so as to insure a restful night. While anodyne cough-medicine often destroys appetite and digestion, it is also true that the cough may be so severe as to provoke gagging and even vomiting, and may thus interfere greatly with the maintenance of nutrition. There are, therefore, times when the cough of consumption should receive special treatment, and times when such treatment is detrimental. The physician is often told by his consumptive patient that if only his cough was stopped he would feel quite well. This is true, providing the cough ceases because the disease disappears, but it is not true if the cough is only suppressed by an anodyne cough-medicine. The severity and frequency of coughing is not a criterion of the gravity of the disease.

Coughing often occurs severely in paroxysms which recur in individual cases at certain times in the day. Most patients cough often in the evening, and, if not then, at bed-time. They are frequently awakened at night in order to cough. A hard spell of coughing is usual when a consumptive wakens, and expectoration is more abundant than at any other time in the day.

Severe coughing in the evening is frequently due to exhaustion. Those who are troubled by it should retire early,—by eight or nine, or even earlier. They often sit up purposely as late as possible because of the coughing and an inability to get to sleep. This is an error in the conduct of their life. They should retire earlier instead of later, and should be careful during the day not to become too fatigued. Evening coughing is also aggravated by sitting for several hours in family-rooms with many others, where the air becomes close, overheated, and often filled with tobacco-smoke, or other irritating fumes, and where the invalid, though tired, is tempted to talk. The early evening should be passed in a quiet room, the air of which is kept clear. Much conversation should not be indulged in at this hour.

Coughing when a patient first lies down is often severe, and may last for hours. It may be due to several causes, or to their simultaneous action. The patient is usually wearied, and, under such circumstances, coughing is easily excited. The exertion of going to one's bed-room and hastily disrobing is considerable. A sudden change in the position of the body, from the upright to the reclining, is sometimes a sufficient cause of coughing. A bed-room may be cold, or cooler than the invalid has been used to during the few preceding hours. The breathing of colder air may provoke the cough. Oftenest several of these causes act coincidently. I need hardly say the air of the bed-room should be properly tempered, and, if necessary, the bed should be warmed. If a patient must climb stairs to reach his bed-room, it should be done so slowly that he will not feel at all breathless when the top is reached. When necessary, he should rest on the way. Clothing should not be removed at once, but a rest of a quarter- or half-hour should be taken in a chair. He should then undress leisurely. Individuals who are weak often exercise more violently while removing and getting into clothing than at any other time in the day. They should be assisted. The arms ought not to be suddenly raised or jerked. Nor ought the body to be violently bent and twisted. The motions should be made slowly, and frequent rests of several minutes' duration should be taken. When finally prepared for bed, the invalid who is troubled with severe coughing at this time ought not suddenly to lie down. He should at first sit up in bed for a minute or two, and then lie semi-recumbent upon pillows, and very slowly and gradually, during a half-hour or so, lower his head to a position that is comfortable for sleeping.

It must not be supposed that these directions will enable every consumptive to avoid evening or bed-time cough. Often, if faithfully executed, they will lessen its severity and its duration, and sometimes will prevent it. Severe cases require also an anodyne cough-medicine at night.

Coughing in the night is usually due to the accumulation of secretions in the air-passages until they must be expelled. If, when a patient awakes, he coughs, expectorates, and falls readily asleep again, the cough is rather beneficial than harmful. If coughing is hard and prolonged at these times, it should be ameliorated. Weakness often makes it hard. When this is the case a little warm food will frequently lessen its severity and duration. A cup of warm cocoa or milk or gruel is the best. Less frequently cold drinks will answer as well as warm. These substances help to give needed strength, and the warm liquids help to loosen the expectoration and make at least the nerves in the throat less irritable. Many times coughing occurs more quickly if the invalid lies more upon one side than the other. These differences should be noted; and when sleep is sought, the position should be assumed in which it can be had most restfully.

A spell of coughing in the morning, either on awakening or arising, is the rule with consumptives in whom the disease is active. It is caused by an accumulation of secretions in the air-passages. These must be gotten rid of, and anodynes to prevent coughing are, therefore, not indicated. The attempt should rather be to give the patient strength to bear the coughing spell, or to make it effective, and such drugs should be used as will make the secretions to be expectorated thinner and more easily dislodged.

An early breakfast will help to give or conserve strength. It may be made of a cup of cocoa and bread or toast, or a glass of milk with bread, or a custard of egg and milk. It should be given as soon as the invalid awakes. Warm food often makes the coughing easier, but its chief purpose is to give strength both to make it bearable and efficient. This little breakfast should not displace a later one. The morning cough can be helped by appropriate medicine when it is severe.

A much more difficult coughing spell to manage is that which occurs immediately after meals. It often provokes vomiting, which causes a loss of necessary nourishment. Frequently persistent irritation of the pharynx by coughing causes the latter to become so sensitive that the swallowing of food provokes coughing and even vomiting. This form of cough can sometimes be helped by remedies applied locally to the throat. If food is taken in a liquid form the cough and vomiting can occasionally be prevented. In many troublesome cases I have seen the difficulty abated by the administration of food in small amounts at frequent intervals. More rarely coughing will not be provoked if the invalid eats in a recumbent or semi-recumbent posture.

These forms of paroxysmal coughing are most apt to occur in those in whom the disease has caused much weakness. They rarely are noticeable in its early stages.

Many consumptives experience no pain, but

this is not the rule. Pain in the chest is of common occurrence. It may be due to neuralgia, to rheumatism, and to pleurisy. The latter is the commonest cause. It is usually aggravated by deep breathing and by coughing. Often it is so slight or temporary that it requires no special treatment. In other cases it is so severe or so frequent in occurrence that it demands the physician's attention. Not unfrequently I am asked what can be done to relieve these severe but transitory pains when medical aid is not at hand. Heat usually affords prompt relief, but if the pain is very sharp, counter-irritation, which can be produced by a small blister, can be relied upon with much confidence. Heat is easiest applied by means of a poultice. It should be applied as hot as possible, and, unless the pain disappears with great promptness, should be renewed often enough to keep it hot. A mustard-plaster will accomplish the same purpose. If a blister is necessary, a small one is usually all that is needed. A piece of Spanish-fly plaster an inch square, if applied directly over the most painful spot, will usually give relief as promptly and perfectly as one three times as large. Rest is essential to relieve these pains, for it aids one to avoid deep breathing and muscular movements, which aggravate them. It is, by all means, best to call upon a physician for counsel in all such attacks.

Another source of much annoyance is found in the night-sweating which accompanies consumption. It causes much discomfort, and is sometimes so profuse as to cause weakness. The sweats are almost uniformly less when moderate exercise and an abundance of out-door air can be had than when the invalid is confined to the house by inclement weather or weakness. When not profuse they can often be checked by bathing the entire body with tepid or cold water before retiring. In some instances salt-water baths, and, still more frequently, alcohol and vinegar baths, prove efficacious. When night-sweating occurs only in the early morning, if a glass of milk is taken an hour or two before it is expected, it can often be lessened or avoided. If night-sweats are not copious or constant in their recurrence, they do not require especial treatment. The patience and ingenuity of the physician is often taxed to devise means for their suppression.

Hæmorrhage from the lungs usually causes unnecessary alarm. It is rarely so profuse as to endanger life, or even to cause weakness. In most instances only a few mouthfuls of clear blood are expectorated. If such a hæmorrhage occurs for the first time it may rightly be looked upon with dread, for, while not producing fatal results, it means, almost without exception, that consumption has attacked that person's lungs. These slight hæmorrhages may recur often. Hæmorrhages may occur before any sign of the disease can be discovered by the most careful examination. They may occur at any stage of its progress. The dangerously profuse bleedings are usually associated with the occurrence of lung-cavities.

To check hæmorrhages, bodily rest is essential, and, if the bleeding has been severe, should be maintained for some time after it has ceased. Cold drinks and pieces of ice, allowed to melt in the mouth or to be swallowed slowly, aid in checking the flow of blood. Warm drinks should be avoided, and, in profuse hæmorrhages, even warm food. An ice-bag may be applied to the chest with advantage. Severe coughing should be checked. Salt-water gargles and drinks are often resorted to with benefit, but it is doubtful if with more benefit than can be derived from cold drinks and ice. A physician should always be consulted when a hæmorrhage occurs. The directions that I have given are always applicable until his advice can be had.

EVIDENCES OF IMPROVEMENT.

A gain in flesh is the evidence of improvement which is most to be welcomed. A steady gain in weight may rightly give one a confident hope of renewed health. It is important to note the consumptive's weight from week to week in order thoroughly to appreciate the tendencies of the disease in a given case. It is true that sometimes increase of weight will occur while the fever remains high and while signs of serious trouble exist, but usually with such a gain all the symptoms lessen in severity and with a persistent gain successively disappear.

A greater lung-capacity is another evidence of marked improvement. This change is especially to be looked for and hoped for in those predisposed to the disease or suffering from it in its incipiency or from it in its most chronic form. It means that the tendency of the disease to contract the lungs, and thereby lessen their capacity, is counteracted and a normal amount of air-space is being gained.

The lung-capacity is best tested with the spirometer, which measures the amount of air that can be breathed out after as full an inflation of the lungs as is possible. By measuring the girth of the chest at the nipple-line when the chest is as perfectly emptied as possible, and again when filled to its fullest extent, its relative capacity can be roughly determined. But small variations in respiratory capacity cannot be thus determined. An increase in girth is always favorable, especially if the increase takes place upon both sides of the chest. Those whose chests are being enlarged by pulmonary gymnastics will not so soon notice an increased difference in girth where exhalation is complete and inhalation full as an increase during quiet or normal exhalation and inhalation. This is because a habit of deeper and more perfect breathing is acquired before time enough has elapsed to make it possible to materially enlarge the chest.

When deeper breathing becomes a habit, respiration also becomes slower. It is, therefore, a sign of improvement. Under these circumstances the pulse becomes slower and its retardation is also significant of improvement. Fever may quicken both the pulse and respiration, in spite of increased lung-capacity, but the latter change can rarely be effected while fever is continuous. If an abnormally high temperature occurs irregularly, changes in the average rate of respiration and pulse must be sought for evidence of improvement. The disappearance of fever is a very important sign of improvement. An irregular rise of temperature, especially one that occurs only once in two or three days, is comparatively favorable. The height of temperature is not as indicative of an unfavorable course as is the persistence of fever throughout the twenty-four hours and day after day. Usually before the fever of consumption disappears it becomes more and more irregular in its course, and longer periods of normal temperature occur.

One of the last symptoms to disappear is cough. Its severity may vary greatly at any time, but it will not entirely disappear unless active inflammation of the lungs has entirely subsided.

Therefore, in watching for signs of improvement in a consumptive in the midst of the disease, we expect to notice longer periods of low temperature and increased weight, then slower pulse, and, when a period of quiescence is fairly established, habitually deeper breathing and entire absence of fever; finally, a gradual enlargement of the chest and disappearance of cough. The failure to refer here to the medicinal treatment of consumption may create the belief that I think it useless. This is not true. It is necessary, but it must be adapted to each symptom as it arises. Of all diseases, consumption, for its successful treatment, especially requires close and prolonged watching by medical men. It is an exceedingly chronic disease, and its victims should be kept under treatment, and held rigidly to a proper course of life, not for months only, but for years. The best treatment and advice will be obtained if the consumptive will place himself in the hands of a physician upon whom he can rely, who will carefully study his case and guide him. During periods of quiescence in the disease, and when it causes the least inconvenience, the most can be accomplished toward restoring the lungs to a healthy condition; but these are times when, from a notion of false economy, the physician is forsaken, and his advice is neither sought nor regarded. Frequent changes from the care of one physician to another is detrimental, as it prevents their becoming thoroughly acquainted with the individual case and their directing a systematic course of treatment, since it must be planned to extend over months or years.

DURATION OF CONSUMPTION.

Consumption is pre-eminently a chronic disease. Cases are numerous in which it has existed for very many years. The average duration, as it is generally stated, is not great. Twenty-four to thirty-six months are the average limits that are usually given. This average is arrived at by a study of hospital cases. These are drawn almost exclusively from the poorer classes, who are unable to seek a physician or care for themselves systematically in the early stages of the disease. It therefore runs an accelerated course. Almost all observers who gather their statistics from private practice assign a much greater average duration to the disease. Such statistics are, however, not numerous. In this latter class of cases the average is from six to eight years. They comprise persons in whom the existence of the disease is recognized in its incipiency, and who are most persistent in carrying out both hygienic and medicinal treatment. The most extensive and carefully-studied statistics of this class that have come under my observation were collected by Dr.

Williams, of London. Of 1000 of his private patients whose career was watched for a series of years, he found 802 living when the statistics were analyzed; of these, 46 per cent. were cured; 38 per cent. were greatly improved, in 13.4 per cent. the disease was stationary, and in 43.5 per cent. there was increase of trouble. Of the 1000, 198 died, but the average duration of their life was 7 years 8.7 months; 64 per cent. of these lived more than 5 years. Of those alive when the statistics were tabulated, 41.4 per cent. lived from 1 to 5 years, 58.6 per cent. lived 5 years and more, and 30 per cent. lived from 10 to 30 years. These facts emphasize the chronic character of the disease when it is well cared for.

Thirty-five per cent. so far recovered that they could return to and pursue their regular occupations and maintain so good general health that they might be considered well. Those who were worse, and must be looked upon as genuine invalids, constituted only 28 per cent. Dr. Williams concludes, from his statistics, that "surely the time is come when we can hold out a fairly hopeful future to the consumptive patient. We can tell him that if he is prepared to make certain sacrifices of time, of money, and of liberty for some years, to rigidly carry out certain common-sense rules which long experience of the disease inculcates, he may, under favorable circumstances, live for a long period, even to the ordinary span of life; and, as he lives on, may gain sufficient strength to resume his former occupation and duties."

Although no observing physician doubts the efficacy of good hygiene in prolonging the life of consumptives, and in preventing the development of the disease in those disposed to it, it is difficult to find statistics which will throw light upon the matter. A valuable lesson is, however, taught by comparing the statistics gathered by a Royal Commission of 1857 in England to investigate the unusual mortality in the army of that country with similar statistics collected in recent years. In her Majesty's Foot-Guards there was found to be from all causes a mortality of 20 per 1000; from consumption alone 11.4, which was more than the total mortality of the civil male population of England at the same age. In the army, generally, the mortality from consumption was 7.8 per 1000. Since the great mortality was pointed out, great care has been taken to insure more space in barrack-rooms and a certain standard of air-renewal. The result has been that the mortality has been reduced to 2.5 per 1000, which is almost as low as the mortality in the healthiest districts of England. These figures teach us the importance of ventilation. We cannot but wonder what might be accomplished if the same reforms that were affected in the construction of barracks could be effected in house, factory, and counting-room construction. We must feel convinced that by such changes alone the enormous mortality now existing the world over from consumption could be greatly lessened.

It is not possible, by any means with which we are now acquainted, to eradicate the disease from the world; but if all who are predisposed were shown their danger, and instructed in regard to the means by which it could be averted, it would require not more than one or, at most, two generations to reduce its mortality as much as vaccination has reduced the mortality of small-pox.

I need hardly again in this essay plead for the systematic, careful, physical examination, training, and instruction of children and youths of all classes. Such oversight and education is as essentially a part of the duties of the State as it is to insure each child a simple education in letters. An ability to read is not more essential to good citizenship than an ability to maintain health.

www.ingramcontent.com/pod-product-compliance
Lightning Source LLC
Chambersburg PA
CBHW030343170426
43202CB00010B/1227